P9-CER-107

Sports Illustrated KIDS

BIG BOOK OF WHO

ALL-STARS

Sports Illustrated Kids

Managing Editor and Publisher Bob Der
Creative Director Beth Power Bugler
Project Editor Andrea Woo
Director of Photography Marguerite Schropp Lucarelli
Photo Editor Annmarie Avila

Created by 10Ten Media

Managing Director Scott Gramling
Creative Director Ian Knowles
Senior Designer Elizabeth Flach
Senior Editor Steven Bennett
Writers Sam Barclay, Tim Gramling
Assistant Editors Zachary Cohen, Nina Pantic
Reporter Corinne Cummings

Time Home Entertainment

Publisher Jim Childs
Vice President, Brand & Digital Strategy Steven Sandonato
Executive Director, Marketing Services Carol Pittard
Executive Director, Retail & Special Sales Tom Mifsud
Executive Publishing Director Joy Bomba
Director, Bookazine Development & Marketing Laura Adam
Vice President, Finance Vandana Patel
Associate Publishing Director Megan Pearlman
Assistant General Counsel Helen Wan
Assistant Director, Special Sales Ilene Schreider
Senior Book Production Manager Susan Chodakiewicz
Brand Manager Jonathan White
Associate Prepress Manager Alex Voznesenskiy
Assistant Brand Manager Stephanie Braga

Editorial Director Stephen Koepp
Senior Editor Rob D'Angelo
Copy Chief Rina Bander
Design Manager Anne-Michelle Gallero
Editorial Operations Gina Scauzillo

Special thanks: Katherine Barnet, Brad Breston, Jeremy Biloon, Dana Campolattaro, Rose Cirrincione, Natalie Ebel, Assu Etsubneh, Mariana Evans, Christine Font, Susan Hettleman, Hillary Hirsch, David Kahn, Amy Mangus, Kimberly Marshall, Nina Mistry, Dave Rozzelle, Ricardo Santiago, Adriana Tierno

Copyright © 2014 Time Home Entertainment Inc.
Published by Time Home Entertainment Inc.
135 West 50th Street
New York, NY 10020

All rights reserved. No part of this book may be reproduced in any form or by any electronic or mechanical means, including information storage and retrieval systems, without permission in writing from the publisher, except by a reviewer, who may quote brief passages in a review.

ISBN 10: 1-61893-107-5
ISBN 13: 978-1-61893-107-8
Library of Congress Control Number: 2014934081

Sports Illustrated Kids if a trademark of Time Inc.

We welcome your comments and suggestions about Sports Illustrated Kids Books. Please write to us at:
Sports Illustrated Kids Books
Attention: Book Editors
P.O. Box 11016
Des Moines, IA 50336-1016

If you would like to order any of our hardcover Collector's Edition books, please call us at 1-800-327-6388 (Monday through Friday, 7 a.m. to 8 p.m., or Saturday, 7 a.m. to 6 p.m., central time).
1 QGT 14

Welcome

Who is the most decorated Olympic athlete ever? Who is the only rookie to win an NBA Finals MVP award? Who is the only player to appear in both a World Series and a Super Bowl? This book answers those questions and many more about the world's greatest athletes, both past and present. We hope you enjoy reading about them as much as you enjoy watching them perform.

Contents

Baseball	4
Basketball	28
Football	52
Golf	76
Hockey	80
Olympics	92
Racing	104
Soccer	108
Tennis	118
Xtreme	122
PLAYER INDEX	126
PHOTO CREDITS	128

BASE

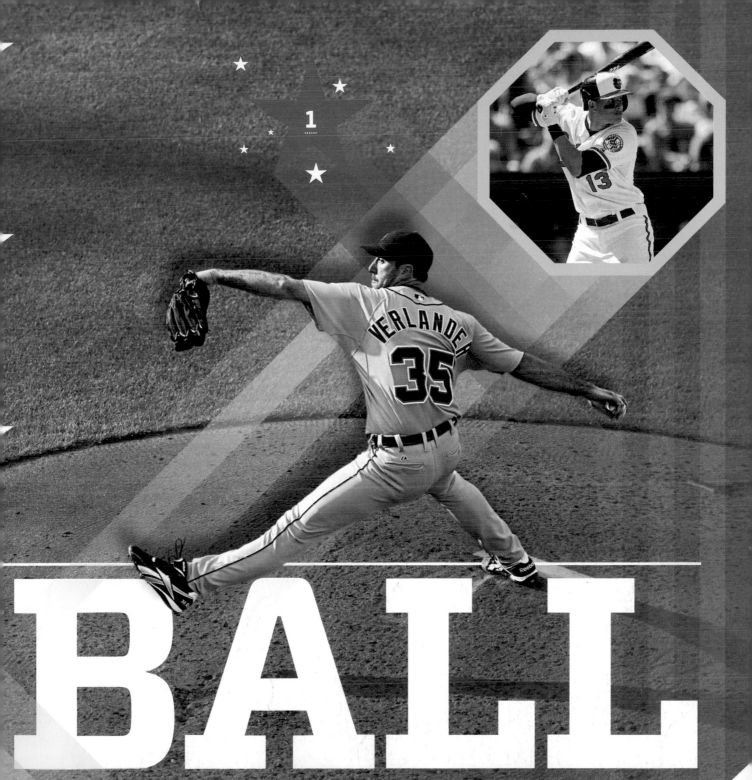

BALL

SUPER STAT:

★ **13** ★

Number of times Rivera was named to Major League Baseball's All-Star Game, which is the most ever for a relief pitcher

Who has the record for most career saves?

During a spectacular career that spanned 19 seasons as a New York Yankee, **Mariano Rivera** set a Major League Baseball record with 652 saves. And that counts only games he saved during the regular season. Rivera saved 42 postseason games in his career, which is also a Major League Baseball record.

Rivera was an inexperienced 19-year-old pitching on a local team in his native Panama when the Yankees signed him. He appeared in his first major league game in 1995 as a starting pitcher, and he was shelled in a 10–0 loss to the California Angels. Rivera posted an ugly 5.94 ERA over 10 starts during that rookie season. That's when the Yankees made the extremely wise decision to move him to the bullpen.

While many great pitchers succeed by keeping hitters off-balance with a variety of pitches, Rivera relied almost entirely on one pitch. That pitch was a cut fastball that darted away from a right-handed batter, or in toward the handle of a lefty's bat. Rivera became famous for using his cut fastball to break the bats of left-handed batters. Before a game in Minnesota during Rivera's final season, the Twins presented the pitcher with a gift they called The Chair of Broken Dreams — a rocking chair made of broken bats. It was a fitting farewell gift for the greatest relief pitcher in baseball history.

Who is the youngest 30/30 player?

Mike Trout of the Los Angeles Angels hit 30 homers and stole 49 bases as a rookie in 2012. Because he didn't turn 21 until August of that season, he became the youngest 30/30 player in major league history. Trout was considered one of the game's top prospects and a future star, but nobody imagined he would become a superstar as quickly as he did. Trout ended up leading the majors in both runs scored (129) and stolen bases as a rookie. He was a unanimous selection as the American League Rookie of the Year.

Who is the Hall of Fame slugger that once led his league in ERA?

Most fans know **Babe Ruth** was one of the greatest hitters in baseball history — he's one of only three players to hit more than 700 career home runs. But not everyone realizes what a great pitcher Ruth was in his six seasons with the Boston Red Sox.

The Red Sox valued Ruth's pitching more than his hitting when he reached the majors. His best season on the mound came when he led the American League with a 1.75 ERA and nine shutouts in 1916. He hit three home runs in limited at bats and didn't give up any homers as a pitcher. In 1918 and '19, Boston started playing Ruth in the field when he wasn't pitching — he led the league in homers both seasons. Before the 1920 season, Boston owner Harry Frazee sold Ruth to the New York Yankees, who wanted him as an outfielder. Frazee's sale remains one of the worst decisions in sports history.

Who is the only player to appear in both a World Series and a Super Bowl?

Deion Sanders was one of the flashiest and most electrifying athletes of the 1990s. He was a football superstar, an excellent baseball player, and a colorful character on and off the field.

Sanders began his baseball career in 1989 with the New York Yankees. His best season was 1992, when he batted .304 and led the National League with 14 triples as an outfielder for the Atlanta Braves. He was a big reason why Atlanta reached the World Series that season.

Meanwhile, Sanders was enjoying even greater success as an NFL cornerback. After five seasons with the Atlanta Falcons, he signed a one-year contract with the San Francisco 49ers in 1994. He was the 1994 NFL Defensive Player of the Year, and he intercepted a pass in the 49ers' Super Bowl XXIX victory.

SUPER STAT:

.533

The batting average Sanders posted in four games during the 1992 World Series despite playing with a broken bone in his foot

SUPER STAT:

.348

Batting average Cabrera posted in 2013 to become the first American Leaguer in 25 years to win three straight batting titles

FAST FACT:

BY WINNING MVP AWARDS IN 2012 AND '13, MIGUEL CABRERA BECAME THE FIRST BACK-TO-BACK AMERICAN LEAGUE MVP SINCE FRANK THOMAS OF THE CHICAGO WHITE SOX IN 1993 AND '94.

Who is the last player to win baseball's Triple Crown?

In 1966, Baltimore Orioles star Frank Robinson led the American League in batting average, home runs, and RBIs, capturing the 14th Triple Crown in major league history. The following season, Carl Yastrzemski of the Boston Red Sox won the 15th. No one would have believed it at the time, but it would be 45 years until another member joined the club, when Detroit Tigers third baseman **Miguel Cabrera** accomplished the feat in 2012.

Cabrera hit .330 to edge out the Los Angeles Angels' Mike Trout for the AL batting title; he drove in 139 runs, 11 more than Josh Hamilton of the Texas Rangers; and he smacked 44 home runs, one ahead of New York Yankee Curtis Granderson.

Cabrera became a star almost immediately after his major league debut as a 20-year-old in 2003. He topped 30 home runs in each of his first two full seasons, becoming the youngest player ever to do so. He was traded to the Tigers prior to the 2008 season, where he continued to dominate at the plate. Cabrera led the American League in home runs in 2008, in RBIs in 2010, and in batting average in 2011 before putting it all together in his remarkable 2012 season.

FAST FACT:
JOE MAUER IS THE ONLY
CATCHER EVER TO WIN
AN AMERICAN LEAGUE
BATTING TITLE.

Who is the catcher with the most batting titles?

Before he moved to first base prior to the start of the 2014 season, **Joe Mauer** of the Minnesota Twins became the only catcher to win three batting titles. The first time he did it, he became the first catcher ever to lead the major leagues in batting average — Mauer's .347 average in 2006 was higher than anyone else in the American League or National League. He then won back-to-back American League batting titles in 2008 and '09. He was named 2009 AL MVP.

It's not often that a player becomes a superstar in his hometown, but that's what Mauer has done. As a high schooler in St. Paul, Minnesota, Mauer struck out only once in four years while hitting higher than .500 every season. He did it while attending high school only seven miles from the Twins' home park, and he was a huge Twins fan growing up. The Twins had the first pick in the 2001 Major League Baseball Draft and they selected their hometown prospect. Three batting titles later, the team's fans are certainly glad they did.

Who was the MVP of the last World Baseball Classic?

The Dominican Republic won all eight games the team played in the 2013 World Baseball Classic. In those eight games, second baseman **Robinson Cano** batted .469 with two home runs and six RBIs, which earned him tournament MVP honors.

The World Baseball Classic was established by professional leagues from around the world to crown a world champion, similar to how the World Cup does for soccer. Whereas the Baseball World Cup and Olympic baseball (which has recently been phased out of the Olympics) feature college and minor league players, rosters in the World Baseball Classic are filled with stars from Major League Baseball.

Cano has been one of baseball's best second basemen since becoming a New York Yankee in 2005. After batting .309 with 204 homers over nine seasons with the Yankees, he joined the Seattle Mariners prior to the 2014 season.

SUPER STAT:

★ **12** ★

Number of homers Cano hit in the final round of the 2011 Major League Baseball Home Run Derby, the highest total ever for a final round

SUPER
STAT:

★ **44** ★

Puig's number of hits in June 2013,
the second-most ever for a debut
month behind Joe DiMaggio's
48 as a New York Yankee
in May 1936

Who had the best debut month in MLB history?

In June 2013, **Yasiel Puig** of the Los Angeles Dodgers went from minor league prospect to major league superstar more quickly than anyone ever has. His first month in the majors was full of memorable moments and remarkable feats. Puig batted .436 with seven home runs, 19 runs, 16 RBIs, and four stolen bases in 26 games during his first month in Los Angeles. His play provided a spark for a team that had been struggling before his arrival.

In his first game with the Dodgers on June 3, 2013, Puig collected two hits against the San Diego Padres. He was equally impressive in the field as he was at the plate. On the final play of the game, Puig caught a fly ball at the warning track in right field. He then threw a perfect strike about 250 feet in the air all the way to first base for a double play when the Padres' baserunner didn't get back to the base in time. The next day, Puig flashed his power and hit home runs in back-to-back innings to help the Dodgers to a comeback win. He then blasted a grand slam in his fourth game — by then, Puigmania was sweeping L.A.

Who has the highest single-round score in an MLB Home Run Derby?

Josh Hamilton stole the show at the Home Run Derby in 2008, which was the outfielder's first season as a Texas Ranger. An amazing 28 of the 38 swings he took in the first round resulted in balls that sailed over Yankee Stadium's outfield wall. At one point, he bashed home runs on 13 straight swings. Hamilton, who now plays for the Los Angeles Angels, was the first overall pick by the Tampa Bay Rays in the 1999 Major League Baseball Draft. His best season was 2010, when he was named American League MVP after slugging 32 home runs while leading the league with a .359 batting average. Hamilton's efforts helped the Rangers to the first World Series appearance in the team's history.

Who was the youngest ever All-Star batter?

Less than 11 weeks after making his debut with the Washington Nationals on April 28, 2012, outfielder **Bryce Harper** was named to the National League All-Star team. Only 19 years old at the time, he became the youngest position player ever to appear in an All-Star Game when he walked as a pinch-hitter to lead off the fifth inning. Harper was named NL Rookie of the Year after ending his first season with 22 home runs and 98 runs scored.

Who is the last catcher to win a batting title?

Buster Posey of the San Francisco Giants had one of the best seasons ever for a catcher in 2012. Not only did he win the National League batting title with a .336 average, but he also hit 24 home runs and drove in 103 to earn NL Most Valuable Player honors. He made the season even more memorable when he helped his Giants to a four-game sweep of the Detroit Tigers to win the 2012 World Series.

Although Posey was only 25 years old in 2012, he went into the season with a lot of valuable experience in big games. After batting .305 with 18 home runs in 2010 to win that season's NL Rookie of the Year award, he excelled in the postseason to take his place as one of baseball's best catchers. Posey batted .375 in the Giants' National League Divisional Series win over the Atlanta Braves. He then became the first rookie with four hits in a NL Championship Series game when he did so in Game 4 against the Philadelphia Phillies. Posey's .300 batting average over five World Series games against the Texas Rangers helped the Giants win their first World Series since 1954.

SUPER STAT:

.433

Posey's batting average against left-handed pitchers in 2012, which was the highest mark among players in Major League Baseball

SUPER STAT:

.321

The career batting average
Jeter has posted with 50
hits in 156 at-bats over
38 career World
Series games

FAST FACT:

NOT ONLY IS DEREK JETER BASEBALL'S
ALL-TIME LEADER IN POSTSEASON HITS,
BUT HE ALSO HOLDS THE RECORDS FOR MOST
GAMES PLAYED, RUNS SCORED, AND TOTAL
BASES IN POSTSEASON HISTORY.

Who has the most career postseason hits in baseball history?

When New York Yankees shortstop **Derek Jeter** lined a single to right field against the Detroit Tigers during the second inning of Game 1 of the 2012 American League Championship Series, it was the 200th hit of his postseason career. No other active player has reached even 90 postseason hits. It's very possible that Jeter may forever reign as the all-time leader in postseason hits.

Former pitcher Hal Newhouser was working as a scout for the Houston Astros when Jeter was a star in high school. Newhouser begged the Astros to take Jeter with the first pick of the 1992 Major League Baseball Draft. Newhouser told the team that he thought Jeter was "going to be the anchor and the foundation of a winning club." When the Astros passed on Jeter to instead take a player named Phil Nevin, Newhouser quit his job in disgust. Newhouser turned out to be right. The Yankees selected Jeter six picks later, and they have won the World Series five times since.

Who is the only two-sport All-Star?

Many consider **Bo Jackson** to be the greatest athlete in sports history. One of his most memorable moments as an outfielder for the Kansas City Royals came when he led off the bottom of the first inning of the 1989 All-Star Game with a long home run. Jackson was named MVP of the American League's 5–3 victory. Less than 18 months later, he was selected to play in the NFL's Pro Bowl after rushing for 698 yards in 10 games for the Los Angeles Raiders. Jackson became the first athlete named to play in the all-star game of two major sports.

Who has driven in the most career runs in baseball history?

No baseball player produced at such a high level for as long as **Hank Aaron** did over 23 seasons with the Milwaukee Braves, Atlanta Braves, and Milwaukee Brewers. He led the majors in RBIs four times during a 10-year span between 1957 and '66, and his career total of 2,297 RBIs is an all-time major league record.

Aaron is also the sport's all-time leader in both total bases (6,856) and extra-base hits (1,477). Although Hammerin' Hank never hit as many as 50 homers in one season, he did hit 40 or more eight times. On April 8, 1974, Aaron hit the 715th home run of his career to break Babe Ruth's record and become baseball's new home run king.

Who has played in the most consecutive games?

Cal Ripken, Jr. played 20 seasons in the majors — all for the Baltimore Orioles. He was the American League Rookie of the Year in 1982, a World Series champion in 1983, and a two-time AL Most Valuable Player. He won two Gold Gloves and eight Silver Slugger awards. But the defining moment of Ripken's career came on September 6, 1995. That's the day he played in his 2,131st consecutive game to break the record set in 1939 by former New York Yankee great Lou Gehrig.

Ripken didn't sit once he owned the record. He kept playing. And playing. He ultimately pushed the record to 2,632 games before deciding to stay on the bench for the Orioles' final home game of the 1998 season. Ripken retired in 2001 as the undisputed Iron Man of baseball.

SUPER STAT:

★ **19** ★

Number of Major League Baseball All-Star Games in which Ripken appeared, which is the most ever by an American League player

Who was the last pitcher to be named Most Valuable Player?

The season that Detroit Tigers starting pitcher **Justin Verlander** had in 2011 was one of the best by any pitcher in modern baseball history. He won the American League's pitching triple crown, with a 2.40 ERA, 250 strikeouts, and 24 wins (against just five losses). Verlander's win total was the highest in the major leagues since Bob Welch of the Oakland A's went 27–6 in 1990, and it made him an easy choice for the 2011 American League Cy Young Award. It also helped him become the first pitcher voted Most Valuable Player since Oakland's Dennis Eckersley in 1992, and the first starting pitcher to be named MVP since Roger Clemens of the Boston Red Sox in 1986.

Verlander's best performance during his MVP season came on May 7, when he threw a no-hitter against the Toronto Blue Jays. The only Blue Jay to reach base the entire game was catcher J.P. Arencibia, who drew a walk in the eighth inning.

SUPER STAT:

★ **251** ★

Number of innings Verlander pitched in 2011, which was the highest single-season total in the majors since 2004

FAST FACT:
JUSTIN VERLANDER IS THE ONLY AMERICAN LEAGUE
PLAYER EVER TO WIN A ROOKIE OF THE YEAR AWARD,
AN MVP AWARD, AND A CY YOUNG AWARD.

Who is the youngest infielder to hit a postseason home run?

When the Baltimore Orioles ended a 15-year playoff drought by reaching the postseason in 2012, one of the reasons for their success was the play of 20-year-old rookie **Manny Machado.** The third baseman then became the youngest infielder in baseball history to hit a postseason home run — he launched a slider from New York Yankees pitcher Hiroki Kuroda over the fence in left field in the top of the fifth inning of Game 3 of the American League Divisional Series. It was a glimpse of things to come from Machado, who led the AL in doubles (51) and played in the 2013 All-Star Game.

FAST FACT:
NOLAN RYAN WAS 44 YEARS OLD WHEN HE THREW HIS SEVENTH CAREER NO-HITTER.

Who has thrown the most career no-hitters?

Nolan Ryan threw seven no-hitters during his 27-year career with the New York Mets, California Angels, Houston Astros, and Texas Rangers. It is a record that may never be broken — Sandy Koufax threw four no-hitters for the Los Angeles Dodgers in the 1960s, and Bob Feller threw three no-hitters for the Cleveland Indians, in 1940, '46, and '51. But no other pitcher has thrown more than two no-hitters.

Ryan was one of the hardest throwers in baseball history — his fastball regularly reached 100 miles per hour. He is baseball's all-time leader in career strikeouts with 5,714, which is also a record that might never be broken. No other pitcher has ever reached 5,000 career strikeouts, and no pitcher who was active at the start of the 2014 season had reached even 2,500.

Who has the most hits in one season?

Ichiro Suzuki became the first Japanese-born position player to play for a Major League Baseball team when he made his debut for the Seattle Mariners on April 2, 2001. He moved to the U.S. after a nine-year stint with the Orix Blue Wave of the Japanese Pacific League. Ichiro enjoyed immediate success, leading the American League with 242 hits, which was the most ever by a rookie. He also had a .350 batting average and 56 stolen bases to become the first player to lead his league in both categories since Jackie Robinson in 1949.

Ichiro's best season would come three years later, when he won his second American League batting title with a .372 average. His 262 hits that season broke George Sisler's 84-year-old single-season record of 257. Ichiro would go on to lead the majors in hits seven times over his first 10 seasons with the Mariners. He also became the first player to surpass 200 hits in 10 straight years.

SUPER STAT:

★ **225** ★

The number of Ichiro's 262 hits in 2004 that were singles, which broke a major league record that had stood for 106 seasons

SUPER
STAT:

★ 20 ★

Number of Pujols's 49 homers
in 2006 that accounted for a
game-winning RBI, which
broke the single-season
record set in 1962

FAST FACT:

ALBERT PUJOLS IS THE ONLY PLAYER IN
MAJOR LEAGUE BASEBALL HISTORY TO HIT
OVER .300 WITH MORE THAN 30 HOMERS AND
100 RBI IN EACH OF HIS FIRST 10 SEASONS.

Who set a record for most total bases in a World Series game?

Game 3 of the 2011 World Series between the St. Louis Cardinals and Texas Rangers was quite a slugfest. Only once before had a team scored more runs in a World Series game than the 16 the Cardinals scored in their 16–7 victory — 75 years earlier, the New York Yankees beat the New York Giants, 18–4, in Game 2 of the 1936 World Series. Leading the charge for St. Louis was superstar first baseman **Albert Pujols,** who turned in the greatest performance by a hitter in a World Series game. Pujols went 5-for-6 with three home runs, six RBIs, four runs scored, and 14 total bases. He tied the World Series records for hits, homers, RBIs, and runs, and he broke the Series record for total bases.

The Cardinals ended up winning the 2011 World Series in seven games. It would turn out to be the last time Pujols would play for St. Louis — he became a free agent after the season and signed with the Los Angeles Angels. He will forever be remembered by Cardinals fans as one of the greatest players in the team's history.

BASKE

TBALL

SUPER
STAT:

★ **61** ★

Career-high number of
points James scored in a
124–107 win over the
Charlotte Bobcats
on March 3, 2014

FAST FACT:
LEBRON JAMES APPEARED ON THE COVER OF
SPORTS ILLUSTRATED WHEN HE WAS STILL
IN HIGH SCHOOL AND ONLY 17 YEARS OLD.

Who is the last player to be named MVP of both the regular season and NBA Finals in two straight seasons?

After he failed to win a championship in his first eight NBA seasons, **LeBron James** was criticized by people who said he didn't have what it takes to win an NBA title. Nobody says that anymore. In 2011–12, King James won his third regular season MVP award. He had a performance for the ages in Game 7 of the 2012 Eastern Conference Finals, scoring 45 points in a victory over the Boston Celtics to send the Miami Heat to the NBA Finals. He then averaged 28.6 points, 10.2 rebounds, and 7.4 assists as the Heat cruised past the Oklahoma City Thunder in five games — James won his first NBA title and was named Finals MVP.

James was named regular season MVP again in 2012–13. This time, the playoffs were a tougher road. In the NBA Finals, Miami was on the brink of elimination in Game 6 against the San Antonio Spurs. James brought the Heat back by scoring 16 points in the fourth quarter of a comeback, overtime victory. One game later, his 37 points tied the Finals record for most points in a Game 7 win. It clinched a second ring for King James, and it earned him a second Finals MVP award.

Who was the first European-born player to be named MVP of the NBA Finals?

San Antonio Spurs point guard **Tony Parker** has a trademark floating jump shot that is impossible to stop when he's on. During the 2007 NBA Finals, he was on. Parker torched the Cleveland Cavaliers for 24.5 points per game. In a series that included stars such as the Spurs' Tim Duncan and Cleveland's LeBron James, it was Parker who was named Finals MVP, the first European-born player to win the award. (While Parker's father, Tony Sr., grew up in Chicago, Tony Jr. was born and raised in France, where his dad played pro basketball.)

Who scored the most points in one game?

When the New York Knicks faced the Philadelphia Warriors on March 2, 1962, they tried to stop star center **Wilt Chamberlain** by repeatedly fouling him. Chamberlain set an NBA record with 28 made free throws (Adrian Dantley of the Utah Jazz matched the record on January 4, 1984). But that's not the record from that night that anyone remembers. Chamberlain also made 36 of 63 shots from the field. He had 41 points at halftime, 69 after three quarters, and 75 with 10 minutes left in the game. The Knicks triple- and quadruple-teamed Chamberlain, but they couldn't stop him. With 46 seconds left, and all five Knicks covering him, Chamberlain finished off a lob pass for an even 100 points, the most ever in an NBA game.

SUPER STAT:

★ **19** ★

Record number of times Abdul-Jabbar was selected to the NBA All-Star Game

Who has the most points in NBA history?

When Lew Alcindor was at UCLA in the 1960s, the 7' 2" center was so dominant that the NCAA banned dunking. So it was no surprise that, after joining the Milwaukee Bucks as the top pick of the 1969 NBA Draft, Alcindor immediately piled up the points. But you won't find the name "Lew Alcindor" in any record book. That's because the day after leading the Bucks to the 1971 NBA title, Alcindor legally changed his name to **Kareem Abdul-Jabbar** to honor his Muslim faith.

Abdul-Jabbar continued to dominate, first with the Bucks and then after he was traded to the Los Angeles Lakers. Wearing goggles after suffering multiple eye injuries on the court, Abdul-Jabbar played 20 seasons, and he averaged more than 20 points per game in 17 of them. By the end of his career in 1989, he had piled up 38,387 career points. Utah Jazz Hall of Famer Karl Malone, who tallied 36,928 career points, has come closest to catching Kareem.

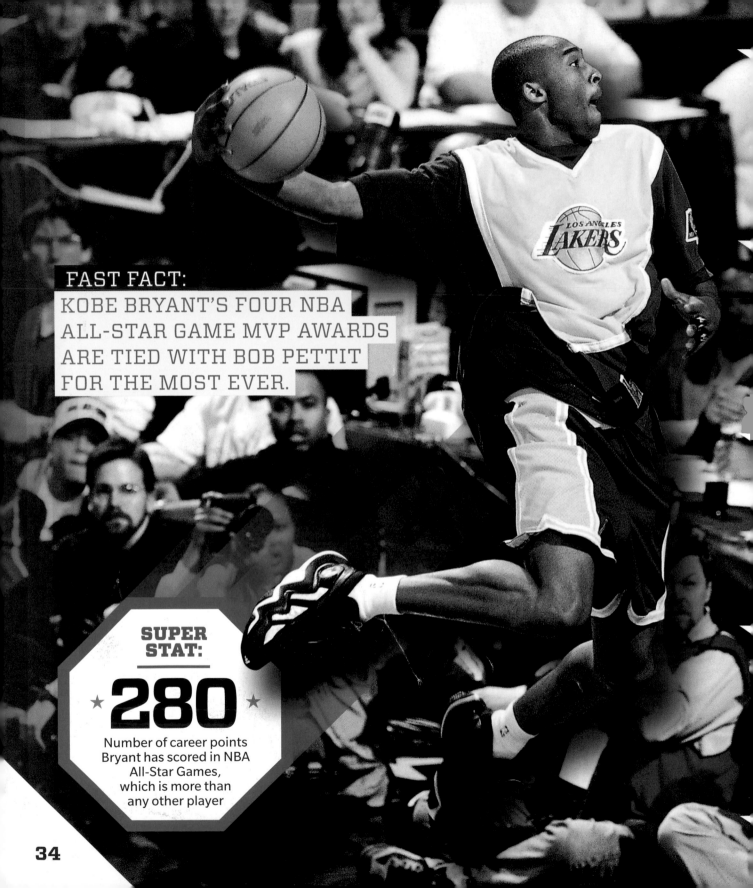

FAST FACT:
KOBE BRYANT'S FOUR NBA ALL-STAR GAME MVP AWARDS ARE TIED WITH BOB PETTIT FOR THE MOST EVER.

SUPER STAT:

★ **280** ★

Number of career points Bryant has scored in NBA All-Star Games, which is more than any other player

Who is the youngest player to win the Slam Dunk Contest?

Before **Kobe Bryant** was a 16-time NBA All-Star, or a five-time NBA champion, or a two-time Finals MVP, he was a teenage sensation. Acquired in a draft day trade with the Charlotte Hornets in 1996 (he was selected 13th overall, and was just 17 years old at the time), the Lakers' rookie sixth man could get a bit out-of-control during games. But one thing he could do early in his career was dunk, and he proved it at the 1997 Slam Dunk Contest in Cleveland, Ohio.

The 18-year-old Bryant squeaked by into the final round of the competition by finishing top three out of six, edging out a field that included fellow rookie Ray Allen. Bryant had been outperformed by veterans Chris Carr and Michael Finley in the first round, but he had saved something special for the final round. Bryant sprinted from half court, leaped, and passed the ball between his legs before throwing down a thunderous one-handed dunk. The crowd erupted, and the judges gave the slam 49 points out of a possible 50. It was enough to make the rookie the Slam Dunk champion. Bryant remains the youngest competitor ever to win the NBA's Slam Dunk competition.

Who has scored the most points in an Olympic game for the U.S.?

He was a New York Knicks superstar who had already won a gold medal with Team USA at the 2008 Olympics. But for the 2012 Games in London, coaches asked **Carmelo Anthony** to come off the bench behind LeBron James and Kevin Durant in order to help team chemistry. Anthony agreed, but the reduced role didn't stop him from lighting it up.

Anthony was the star of the show in the United States' 156–73 victory over Nigeria in the group play round. He scored 37 points and made 10 three-pointers, both Team USA single-game records. Anthony finished as the team's second-leading scorer in the tournament, helping the U.S. go undefeated and win the gold medal for a second straight Olympics.

SUPER STAT:

★ 62 ★

Number of points Anthony scored on January 24, 2004 to set a Knicks record in a 125–96 win over the Charlotte Bobcats

SUPER STAT:

★ **223** ★

Number of blocks Griner had as a freshman in 2009–10, a single-season NCAA Division I record for men or women

Who has the most career blocks in NCAA history?

Of all the great players in the history of college basketball, the most dominant of all time might have been Baylor Lady Bears center **Brittney Griner.** Standing at 6' 8" with long arms and great leaping ability, Griner first became famous for her offensive highlights. Dunks are rare in the women's game, but Griner threw it down more often than any woman ever had; she finished her college career with a record 18 dunks.

But Griner's biggest impact came on defense. As a senior, she broke the NCAA career record for men and women when she swatted her 664th career shot. And that was with two months left in the season. She eventually blew the old record away, finishing her career with 748 blocks. Griner was so dominant that many wondered if she should play in the NBA, rather than the WNBA. Dallas Mavericks owner Mark Cuban even said he'd like to give Griner an opportunity. She stuck with the women's game and became an All-Star for the Phoenix Mercury.

SUPER STAT:

★ 12 ★

Number of consecutive 30-point games Durant had during the 2013–14 season, the NBA's longest 30-point streak since 2003–04

FAST FACT:

KEVIN DURANT WON THE NAISMITH TROPHY AS COLLEGE BASKETBALL'S PLAYER OF THE YEAR IN 2007, THE ONLY SEASON HE PLAYED FOR THE UNIVERSITY OF TEXAS. HE WAS THE FIRST FRESHMAN EVER TO WIN THE AWARD.

Who is the youngest player to win an NBA scoring title?

With his long arms, explosive leaping ability and sweet shooting touch, Oklahoma City Thunder star **Kevin Durant** is thought by many to be the perfect NBA scorer. No one who has tried to guard him would disagree. The soft-spoken Durant was quietly impressive in his first two NBA seasons. He won the league's Rookie of the Year award in 2007–08, and the next season he was one of only six players to average 25 or more points per game.

But his third year, 2009–10, is when Durant really broke out. With the ability to knock down long jump shots, drive past defenders for easy baskets, or draw fouls and get to the free throw line (where he shot 90% that season!), Durant averaged 30.1 points per game. It helped the Thunder improve their record by 27 wins from the previous year, earning them a playoff spot. It also made Durant, then 21 years old, the youngest scoring champion in NBA history. Considering he was at an age when many players are still in college, it's no surprise that Durant has kept piling up the points. He won scoring titles each of the next two seasons as well, establishing himself as one of the top scorers in NBA history.

Who has the most career points in NCAA history?

When **Pete Maravich** played at LSU in the late 1960s, college basketball was a different game. Freshmen were not allowed to play for the varsity team, meaning players got only three years of action. And there was no three-point line. So how did Maravich pile up 3,667 points in his career, more than anyone in college hoops history? By making a ton of shots.

At 6' 5", Maravich had good height for a guard. Nicknamed "Pistol Pete," his skills and creativity as a playmaker made him difficult to defend. As a sophomore in 1967–68, the first season he was eligible to play for the varsity team, he averaged 43.8 points per game. Maravich averaged 44.2 as a junior, and 44.5 as a senior, finishing with a career average of 44.2 points per game. Dale Brown, who later coached at LSU, said he once watched film and charted every shot Maravich took during his LSU career. Brown says that, if the three-point line had been in place when Maravich played, he would have averaged 13 three-pointers per game. That would have raised his career average to an amazing 57 points per game!

SUPER STAT:

★ **28** ★

Number of times Maravich scored 50 or more points in a game for LSU, an NCAA record for most career 50-point games

SUPER
STAT:

★ **39** ★

Number of shots Bogues
blocked during his NBA career,
thanks to his impressive
leaping ability

Who is the shortest player in NBA history?

Basketball is said to be a big man's game at the NBA level. But that doesn't mean the league hasn't had its share of pint-sized stars. The 5' 7" Spud Webb and 5' 9" Nate Robinson were not only solid point guards, but they were Slam Dunk Contest champions as well. Still, neither of them was the shortest player in NBA history. That distinction belongs to **Tyrone (Muggsy) Bogues.**

Standing at just 5' 3", Bogues played 14 seasons for four different NBA teams. He wasn't just a novelty act — Bogues actually used his lack of height to his advantage. He was super-quick, and because he was so low to the ground, he could consistently get into the paint and create chances for teammates. He started more than 500 games during his career, finished in the league's top five in assists in five different seasons, and ranks 17th all-time in career assists (6,726). He could also wreak havoc on the defensive end too. Bogues ranked in the NBA's top 10 in steals three times.

Who is the youngest player ever to be named NBA MVP?

Before the start of the 2010–11 season, everyone wondered who would win NBA MVP. The usual names came up: LeBron James, Kevin Durant, and Kobe Bryant. Chicago Bulls point guard **Derrick Rose** wasn't considered a candidate, but the 22-year-old had other ideas. "Why can't I be the MVP of the league," he asked reporters before the season. The athletic point guard backed up his talk. He averaged 25.0 points and 7.7 assists per game. The Bulls improved by 21 wins and finished with the NBA's best record (62–20). Rose won the MVP vote easily.

Who has won the most NBA championships in league history?

Only one player has more NBA championship rings than he has fingers: **Bill Russell** won 11 NBA titles with the Boston Celtics. He averaged only 15.1 points per game — by comparison, rival Wilt Chamberlain averaged nearly twice that output, 30.1 ppg. But Russell dominated the defensive side of the court like no one ever has. He averaged 22.5 rebounds per game during a 13-year career that began in 1956–57, second all-time only to Chamberlain. And while blocked shots didn't start being kept as a statistic until five years after Russell's final season, there's never been a shot-blocker better than him. He not only erased opponents' shots, but he usually made sure to tip those blocks either to a teammate or to himself, turning them into turnovers rather than simply swatting the ball out of bounds.

Who is the last player to lead all NBA rookies in points and rebounds?

The career of **Blake Griffin** couldn't have gotten off to a worse start. The top pick of the 2009 draft was expected to star immediately for the Los Angeles Clippers. Playing in the final preseason game, he suffered a fractured knee landing after a dunk. It kept him out for the entire season. Because he didn't appear in a regular season game in 2009–10, Griffin was considered a rookie when he took the court in 2010–11. And his strength and explosive leaping ability returned. He even made the Western Conference All-Star team. Griffin finished the season with averages of 22.5 points per game and 12.1 rebounds per game, tops among rookies. He was the unanimous Rookie of the Year.

SUPER STAT:

★ 47 ★

Career-high number of points Griffin scored on January 17, 2011 against the Indiana Pacers, a Clippers record for points by a rookie

SUPER
STAT:

★ **108** ★

NBA record number of
consecutive games in which
Paul had at least one steal,
from April 13, 2007 to
December 23, 2008

Who is the only player to lead the NBA in both assists and steals in two straight seasons?

In the NBA, it's rare that a player who is 6-feet or shorter dominates. That's why, in the 2005 NBA draft, three teams passed on the chance to select Wake Forest point guard **Chris Paul.** The New Orleans Hornets were happy to pick him up fourth overall. At just 6-feet and 175 pounds, Paul may lack size, but he makes up for it with incredible quickness and amazing instincts. He has put those tools to use throughout his career, but especially during the 2007–08 and '08–09 seasons. He led the NBA in both assists (11.6 per game in '07–08, 11.0 per game in '08-09) and steals (2.7 and 2.8) in those two seasons, the only player to lead in both categories in back-to-back years.

The Hornets won just 18 games, fewest in the Western Conference, the season before they drafted Paul. But thanks to their new point guard, they quickly improved to become one of the NBA's top teams. In '07–08, they won their only division title in franchise history, and they nearly upset the mighty San Antonio Spurs in a second-round playoff series. One year later, Paul led them back to the playoffs for a second consecutive season. He was traded to the Los Angeles Clippers prior to the start of the 2010–11 season.

Who was the Heat's first NBA Finals MVP?

Fans are used to seeing LeBron James hold up the Finals MVP trophy when the Miami Heat win it all. But the Heat's first NBA title came before James was on the team, and it was one of his current teammates who led the way. In the 2006 NBA Finals, the Heat lost the first two games to the Dallas Mavericks, and Miami trailed by 13 with less than seven minutes to go in Game 3. That's when **Dwyane Wade** took over. Crashing into defenders as he attacked the basket and piling up points at the free throw line, he scored 15 points in the fourth quarter to finish with 42 for the game. The Heat came back to win Game 3, then the next three games to clinch their first-ever title. Just 24 years old at the time, Wade became the fifth youngest player in league history to be named NBA Finals MVP.

SUPER STAT:

34.7

Wade's average points per game in the 2006 NBA Finals, the third highest scoring by a player in his first NBA Finals

SUPER STAT:

★ 6 ★

Jordan's record number of NBA Finals MVP awards, twice as many as any other player in NBA history

Who scored the most points in one NBA Finals series?

He was the greatest crunch time player the NBA has ever seen, so it makes perfect sense that **Michael Jordan** had the greatest scoring performance in a single NBA Finals series. After winning the 1993 Eastern Conference finals, he advanced to face fellow future Hall of Famer Charles Barkley and the Phoenix Suns. The man known as "His Airness" was up to the task.

After scoring 31 points in Game 1 of the NBA Finals, Jordan went on to score 40 or more in each of the next four games. He's still the only player to ever score 40-plus in four consecutive games in the NBA Finals. His performance in Game 4 of that series was legendary. Jordan poured in 55 points on 21-for-37 shooting, carrying the Bulls to a key victory. He scored "only" 33 in Game 6, but it was enough for the Bulls to clinch the title. He finished the six-game set with a record average of 41.0 points per game.

SUPER STAT:

★ **8** ★

Number of shots Howard blocked in the first half of a playoff win over the Charlotte Bobcats on April 18, 2010, an NBA playoff record

Who is the first player to win three straight Defensive Player of the Year honors?

With the height of a center and quickness of a guard, **Dwight Howard** is one of the NBA's greatest defensive players ever. He was so good on defense that his first team, the Orlando Magic, surrounded him with a group of solid offensive players who couldn't play a lick of D. They knew Howard would erase their defensive mistakes.

Howard is an outstanding shot-blocker, leading the NBA in that category in 2008–09 (2.9 per game) and '09–10 (2.8). He's also the only player to lead the NBA in blocks and rebounds in the same season twice. And he's one of the best ever at defending basketball's most unstoppable play: the pick-and-roll. Howard can move in front of guards until his teammate recovers, then get back and defend his own man again. That rare ability is what helped earn him Defensive Player of the Year honors three seasons in a row, from '08–09 to '10–11.

Who has made the most three-pointers in one season?

Dell Curry was a sharpshooter in the NBA for 16 seasons. But that's nothing compared to what his son has done from behind the arc. The Golden State Warriors' **Stephen Curry** has had the NBA's sweetest shot since he stepped onto the court as a rookie in 2009–10. Among his games was a 54-point performance on the road against the New York Knicks in February 2013. He made 11 threes in that game, one short of the NBA single-game record. He did get into the record book later though. Curry finished the year with 262 makes from behind the arc that season, breaking Ray Allen's single-season record.

Who won the first three Three-Point Shootouts?

Boston Celtics forward **Larry Bird** was a superstar. His best skill was his jump shot, and he had plenty of confidence in it. The NBA held its first All-Star Three-Point Shootout in 1986. In the locker room beforehand, Bird asked the other competitors a question: "Who's finishing second?" He backed up the trash talk. At one point he drained 11 straight shots, and finished with 22 points in the final. He breezed to another Shootout win in 1987. In 1988, Dale Ellis put up a score of 15 points in the final. Bird had 13 points with three balls left. He made two in a row to tie it. He released the final ball and immediately walked away with his index finger raised. Swish. Another win for Larry Legend.

Who is the only rookie to win Finals MVP?

Despite acquiring superstar center Kareem Abdul-Jabbar in a trade before the 1975–76 season, the Los Angeles Lakers had yet to end their championship drought. They needed Magic. The Lakers had acquired a first-round pick from the New Orleans Jazz for the 1979 draft, which ended up being the top pick. They selected **Earvin (Magic) Johnson,** a sophomore from Michigan State. He was the first underclassman ever taken first overall in the NBA draft.

Magic was 6'9", but he had the flashy ball-handling skills and court vision of a point guard. His do-it-all skill set made him an immediate star, and the Lakers' exciting style earned them the nickname "Showtime." Facing the Philadelphia 76ers in the 1980 NBA Finals, L.A. went up 3–2 but lost Abdul-Jabbar to an ankle injury in Game 5. Magic got the start at center in Game 6, and turned in an all-time great performance: 42 points, 15 rebounds, and a perfect 14-for-14 from the foul line. The Lakers clinched the title with a 123–107 win, and Johnson became the first, and still only, rookie to be named Finals MVP.

SUPER STAT:

★ **42** ★

Number of points Johnson scored in Game 6 of the 1980 NBA Finals, the most ever by a rookie in an NBA Finals game

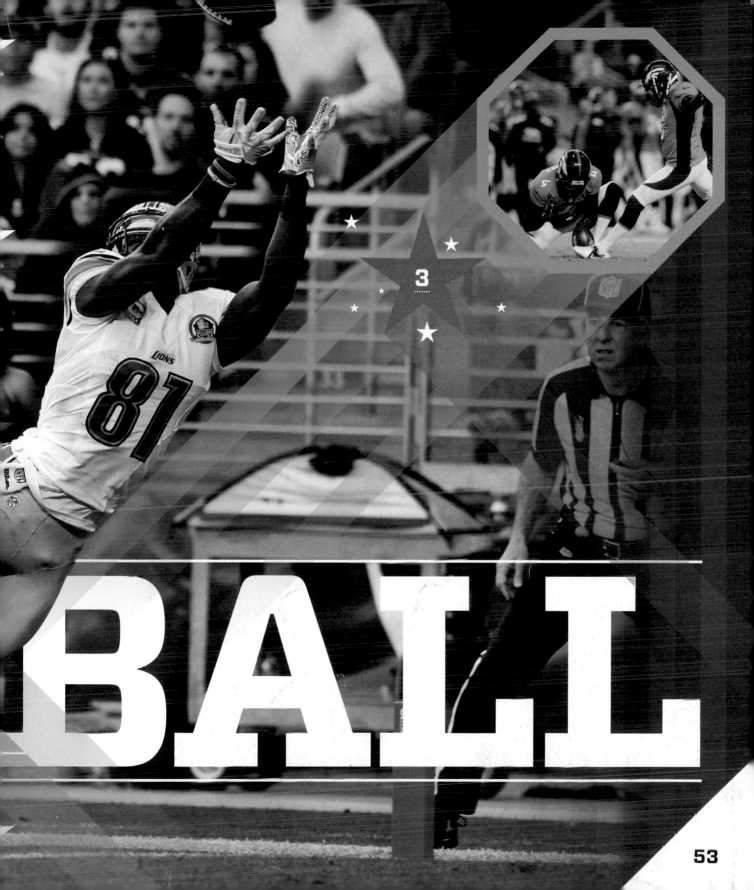

BALL

3

6,589

Manning's number of career passing yards in postseason games, which is the highest total in NFL history

FAST FACT:
PEYTON MANNING
HOLDS THE NFL
RECORD WITH
EIGHT 300-YARD
PASSING GAMES IN
THE POSTSEASON.

Who has won the most NFL MVP awards?

Thirteen trips to the Pro Bowl. Three AFC Championships. A Super Bowl ring. Since entering the league in 1998, **Peyton Manning** has established himself as one of the greatest quarterbacks to ever play the game. He's been named league MVP a record five times. Among active NFL players, only Tom Brady has won the award more than once. (Brady was MVP in 2007 and '10.)

Manning won his fifth MVP in 2013. In the best season ever by a quarterback, he set marks in yards and passing touchdowns, throwing for 55 touchdowns (and running for one more!). Going into the final game of the regular season against the Oakland Raiders, Manning already had 5,211 passing yards on the year, which was behind Drew Brees's 5,476 and Tom Brady's 5,235, both from 2011. Breaking the record proved to be an easy task. Manning threw for 266 yards in the first half, to give him 5,477 yards for the season, before exiting the game at halftime.

Who is the last player to throw seven TD passes in an NFL game?

With seven touchdown passes in a 49–20 blowout victory against the Oakland Raiders on November 3, 2013, Philadelphia Eagles quarterback **Nick Foles** became the seventh NFL player to reach that height — George Blanda, Y.A. Tittle, Sid Luckman, Adrian Burk, Joe Kapp, and Peyton Manning are the others. Foles was as unlikely a candidate as any to join them. He entered the game with six passing TDs for the 2013 season, a number that matched his total for the entire '12 season. Remarkably, Foles finished the day with fewer incompletions (six) than he had touchdown passes, something no other QB tied for the single-game record can claim.

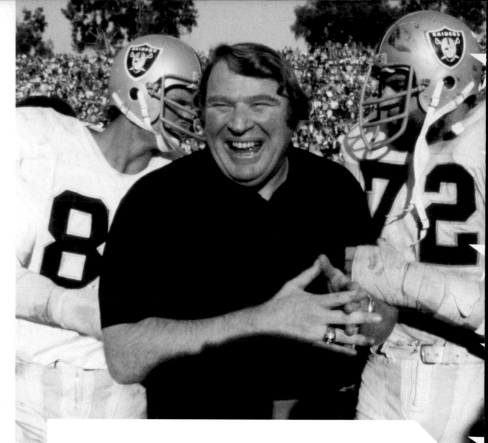

Who inspired the EA Sports *Madden* video games?

What do you think of when you hear the name Madden? The EA Sports football game? The Hall of Fame NFL head coach? Or the long-time NFL broadcaster? No matter which role you associate **John Madden** with, one thing's for sure: He has made his mark on the sport of football.

Madden coached the Oakland Raiders for 10 years from 1969 to '78, and all of them were winning seasons. After leaving coaching at the age of 42, Madden started working as a TV commentator and analyst. In the mid-'80s, while he was working as a broadcaster, Madden consulted on *John Madden Football,* the video game series that later became *Madden NFL.* The first edition came out in 1988 and the game has come a long way since. It is now the best-selling sports video game franchise in North American history.

Who has the most receiving touchdowns by a running back in one game?

After scoring the most touchdowns in the league in 2013, **Jamaal Charles** certainly earned his role as a Pro Bowl captain that season. The Kansas City Chiefs running back had 19 TDs in the regular season, three more than the second-place finisher, New Orleans Saints tight end Jimmy Graham. Charles finished with 12 rushing TDs and seven receiving TDs, proving he's a real double-threat on offense.

He also became the running back with the most receiving touchdowns in one game. In a Week 15 game against the Oakland Raiders, Charles had four receiving touchdowns. (He also scored a rushing touchdown, making him the only player at any position to have four receiving TDs and a rushing TD in a single game.)

SUPER STAT:

★ 162 ★

Number of rushing yards Charles gained against the New Orleans Saints in the third quarter of a game in 2012, the most ever in one quarter

Who has the most receiving yards in one season?

Detroit Lions receiver **Calvin Johnson** is called Megatron for a reason. Like the *Transformers* robot of the same name, he seems superhuman, armed with elite tools that make him the best at his position. Johnson has size (6' 5", 236 pounds); he has speed (a 4.35-second 40-yard dash); he can reach amazing heights, soaring to complete acrobatic receptions; and his hands seem to be made of glue.

It's no wonder that the hard-working Johnson finished the 2012 season with a record 1,964 receiving yards. His 225-yard performance in Week 15 broke Jerry Rice's single-season yards record of 1,848, set in 1995. After the game, Rice told *Sports Illustrated:* "You never want your records to be broken, but if anyone is going to do it, I prefer if Megatron does it."

FAST FACT:
CALVIN JOHNSON'S FIVE GAMES OF 200 OR MORE RECEIVING YARDS ARE TIED FOR THE MOST IN NFL HISTORY.

SUPER STAT:

★ **329** ★

Number of receiving yards Johnson had against the Dallas Cowboys on October 27, 2013, an NFL record for a game that did not go to overtime

Who leads all quarterbacks in career NFL postseason victories?

On January 13, 2013, **Tom Brady** set the record for most playoff wins by a QB when he led the New England Patriots to a 41–28 defeat of the Houston Texans. It was his 17th career postseason victory, breaking the record of 16 set by Joe Montana, who Brady idolized as a kid. Brady extended his postseason win tally to 18 after beating the Colts in the playoffs in January 2014. The Patriots QB has been the driving force behind the team's phenomenal run that started in 2001— through the 2013 season, the Pats have made 11 postseason appearances and won the Super Bowl three times.

SUPER STAT:

92.9%

Percentage of passes Brady completed to set a single-game postseason record against the Jacksonville Jaguars on January 12, 2008

Who is the only defensive player to win the Heisman Trophy?

The Heisman Trophy has been awarded every year since 1935 — but only once has it gone to a defensive player. That man is **Charles Woodson,** who won the award in 1997 for his outstanding season at Michigan, primarily playing the cornerback position. In his junior season, Woodson made eight interceptions and scored three touchdowns during his occasional stints on offense. In one game that year against Ohio State, Woodson returned a punt for a touchdown, made an end zone pick, and caught a 37-yard reception that led to his team's only offensive TD of the day. With Woodson leading the way, Michigan went undefeated that season, won the Rose Bowl, and shared the National Championship.

Woodson continued to be a star after the Oakland Raiders drafted him in 1998. He's played in the Pro Bowl in three different decades — the 1990s, the 2000s, and the 2010s. He signed with the Packers in 2006 and went on to earn a Super Bowl ring after the 2010 season.

SUPER STAT:

★ 13 ★

Woodson's number of career defensive touchdowns entering the 2014 season, which is tied for the most in NFL history

SUPER STAT:

★ 12 ★

Number of career touchdown runs Peterson had of at least 60 yards entering the 2014 season, the most in NFL history

FAST FACT:
ADRIAN PETERSON SET THE NCAA FRESHMAN SINGLE-SEASON RUSHING RECORD WITH 1,925 YARDS IN 2004 AT THE UNIVERSITY OF OKLAHOMA.

Who has the most rushing yards in one NFL game?

It was November 4, 2007. The man with the ball was Minnesota Vikings rookie running back **Adrian Peterson.** And the result was history: On 30 carries against the San Diego Chargers, Peterson ran for 296 yards in one game, the most in NFL history. Peterson averaged 9.9 yards per carry in that game — and he's been nearly unstoppable ever since.

As a boy growing up in Palestine, Texas, Peterson earned the nickname All Day for his relentless energy. The nickname stuck. As defenses get tired late in the game, Peterson seems to run harder than he did on his first carry. His 2012 NFL MVP season was one of the most memorable ever. Coming off a devastating 2011 season-ending knee injury, Peterson ran for 2,097 yards, just eight yards short of Eric Dickerson's record of 2,105 yards in a season by a running back.

Who has the most consecutive games with a touchdown pass?

No NFL quarterback has been more consistent than **Drew Brees** has been for the New Orleans Saints. His streak of throwing at least one touchdown pass in 54 consecutive games is an NFL record. In Week Five of the 2012 season, Brees threw a TD pass to Devery Henderson for his 48th straight game with at least one touchdown, breaking the mark that the legendary Johnny Unitas held for 52 years. Brees extended his streak to 54 games before the Falcons held him TD-less in Week 13.

SUPER STAT:

★ **468** ★

Number of passes Brees completed during the 2011 regular season, which is an NFL record

SUPER STAT:

★ 25 ★

Number of passes Winston completed on 27 attempts in his college debut against Pittsburgh

Who is the youngest player ever to win the Heisman Trophy?

As the quarterback for the Florida State Seminoles during the 2013 regular season, **Jameis Winston** set national freshman records with 3,820 passing yards and 38 touchdowns, finishing the year as the country's leader in passing efficiency. For his dominant year, Winston won the Heisman Trophy as college football's best player at the age of 19 years and 342 days old. He became the youngest player to take home the award and only the second freshman after Texas A&M's Johnny Manziel, who won in 2012.

Winston wasn't finished yet. He celebrated his 20th birthday on January 6, 2014, by throwing a two-yard TD with 13 seconds remaining in the fourth quarter for a dramatic 34–31 win over Auburn in the BCS championship game. He led the Seminoles back from an 18-point deficit to secure their first national title since 1999. The team finished the season with a perfect 14–0 record. That's a pretty good birthday.

Who has the NFL rookie record for most passing yards?

Going into the 2012 NFL draft, many experts thought that Stanford star **Andrew Luck** had the talent to be a franchise quarterback. With the top pick, the Indianapolis Colts took their chance on Luck — and he quickly proved that they made the right choice. Luck threw for 4,374 yards in 2012, more than any rookie in the history of the NFL. He continued his success in 2013, taking the Colts to the playoffs. With Indianapolis trailing by 28 points in a wild card round matchup against the Chiefs, Luck showed his poise and leadership when he led the Colts to a 45–44 comeback win.

Who has scored the most touchdowns in NFL history?

"Touchdown, **Jerry Rice** !" If you watched football in the mid-1980s and '90s, you would have heard commentators yelling that a lot. The reason is simple: With 208 career TDs, the wide receiver was in the end zone more than any player in the history of the game. More amazingly, he broke the record in 1994, the 10th year of his career. Over the next 10 years he continued to add another 81 TDs to his haul.

Rice played for the San Francisco 49ers from 1985 to 2000 and then briefly for the Oakland Raiders and the Seattle Seahawks. His achievements include: 13 Pro Bowls, three Super Bowl rings, and the records for all-time receiving yards (22,895), receptions (1,549), and receiving touchdowns (197).

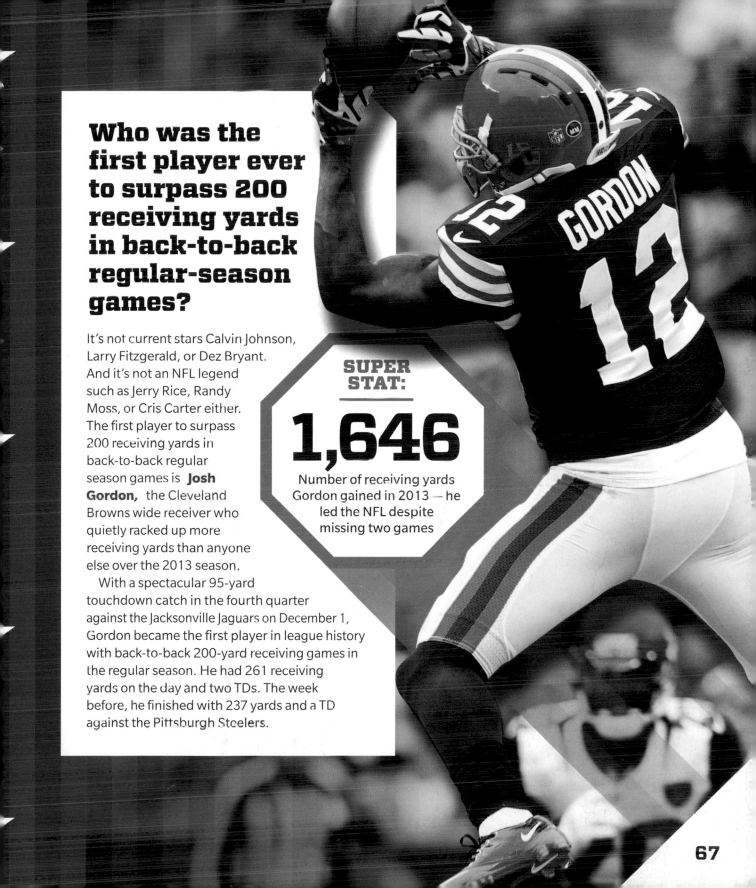

Who was the first player ever to surpass 200 receiving yards in back-to-back regular-season games?

It's not current stars Calvin Johnson, Larry Fitzgerald, or Dez Bryant. And it's not an NFL legend such as Jerry Rice, Randy Moss, or Cris Carter either. The first player to surpass 200 receiving yards in back-to-back regular season games is **Josh Gordon,** the Cleveland Browns wide receiver who quietly racked up more receiving yards than anyone else over the 2013 season.

With a spectacular 95-yard touchdown catch in the fourth quarter against the Jacksonville Jaguars on December 1, Gordon became the first player in league history with back-to-back 200-yard receiving games in the regular season. He had 261 receiving yards on the day and two TDs. The week before, he finished with 237 yards and a TD against the Pittsburgh Steelers.

SUPER STAT:

1,646

Number of receiving yards Gordon gained in 2013 — he led the NFL despite missing two games

Who has kicked the longest field goal in NFL history?

On December 8, 2013, Denver Broncos kicker **Matt Prater** made a 64-yard field goal in front of his home crowd on the last play of the first half against the Tennessee Titans, breaking the record for the longest field goal in NFL history. The previous mark of 63 yards was set in 1970 by New Orleans Saints kicker Tom Dempsey; Jason Elam, Sebastian Janikowski, and David Akers had all matched that 63-yard mark in the past decade.

It's no surprise that the record fell in Denver. Oakland Raiders kicker Janikowski told *Sports Illustrated* in 2012 that he estimates the ball can travel up to as much as seven yards farther at the Broncos' stadium than it does in other arenas. How so? Denver is at 5,280 feet above sea level and the stadium has the highest elevation of any in the NFL. The higher the elevation, the lower the air pressure. The lower the air pressure, the fewer the molecules of nitrogen, oxygen, and other gasses that exist in the air. Molecules create friction, or drag, and that can slow the ball down. So fewer molecules in Denver, plus Matt Prater's boot, and you've got a record-setting field goal.

SUPER STAT:

★ **81** ★

NFL-best number of times Prater forced an opposing team to take a touchback by kicking the ball into or beyond the end zone in 2013

FAST FACT:
THE ONLY KICK MATT PRATER MISSED
DURING THE 2013 REGULAR SEASON WAS A
52-YARD FIELD GOAL ATTEMPT IN WEEK 11.
HE MADE ALL 100 OF HIS OTHER ATTEMPTS:
25 FIELD GOALS AND 75 EXTRA POINTS.

Who has the most rushing yards in a game by a QB?

A dual-threat quarterback, one who can both pass and rush effectively, is one of the greatest weapons a team can have. The San Francisco 49ers have such a talent in their young quarterback, **Colin Kaepernick.** Kaepernick set a single-game NFL record for rushing yards by a quarterback when he ran for 181 against the Green Bay Packers on January 12, 2013, in the divisional round of the playoffs. The 49ers won 45–31, with Kaepernick rushing for two TDs in the game. When he was in the fourth grade, Kaepernick wrote a letter to himself predicting that he would grow up to be between 6' and 6'4" (he's 6'4") and that he would "go to the pros and play on the Niners or the Packers." Not a bad prediction. With Kaepernick's ability to do it all on the field, it's pretty safe to forecast even more records and success in his future.

SUPER STAT:

★ 412 ★

Number of yards Kaepernick passed for in a win over the Packers in the 2013 season opener, the most by a 49er since 2004

SUPER STAT:

★ **156** ★

Number of tackles Kuechly recorded during the 2013 regular season, which led all NFC players for a second straight year

Who is the last NFL player to record more than 20 tackles in one game?

Luke Kuechly was named NFL Defensive Rookie of the Year after leading the league in tackles with 164 in 2012. In 2013, he was named NFL Defensive Player of the Year for his dominant, relentless play. No one would disagree, especially not those who saw his performance in a key game against the NFC South division rival New Orleans Saints with first place on the line in Week 16. Kuechly racked up 24 tackles in the Panthers' 17–13 victory — as many tackles as anyone has had in a game since the NFL began tracking tackles as a stat in 1994. (David Harris of the New York Jets also recorded 24 tackles in a game in 2007.)

What makes Kuechly so good? Watch any of his games and the answer is clear: He's always there, running sideline to sideline from the middle linebacker position to make a play. He's tough against the run and he has the speed and skills to drop back into pass coverage when needed.

71

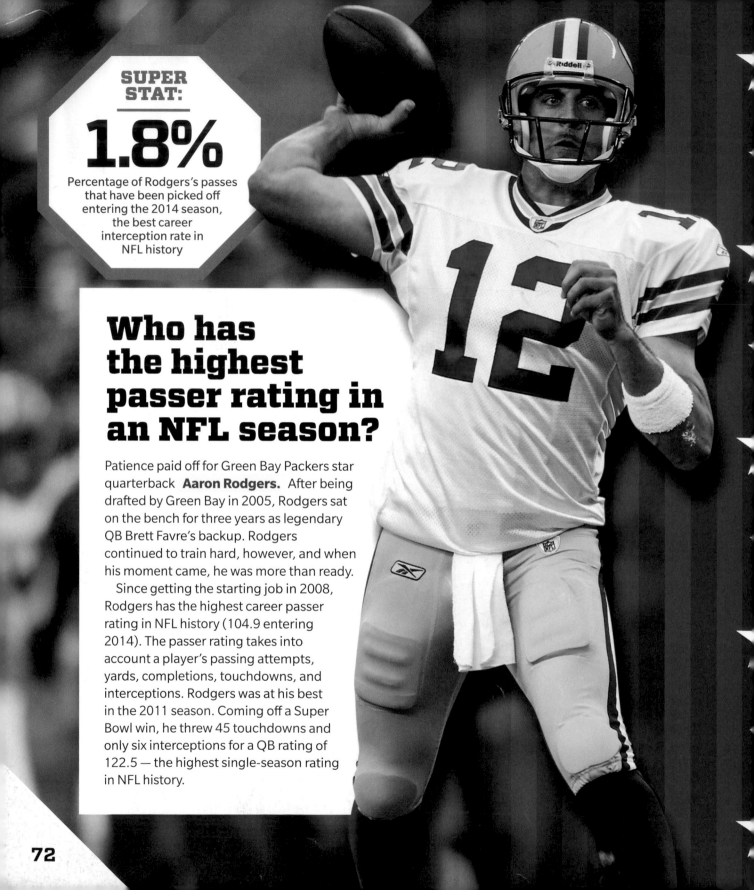

SUPER STAT:

1.8%

Percentage of Rodgers's passes that have been picked off entering the 2014 season, the best career interception rate in NFL history

Who has the highest passer rating in an NFL season?

Patience paid off for Green Bay Packers star quarterback **Aaron Rodgers.** After being drafted by Green Bay in 2005, Rodgers sat on the bench for three years as legendary QB Brett Favre's backup. Rodgers continued to train hard, however, and when his moment came, he was more than ready.

Since getting the starting job in 2008, Rodgers has the highest career passer rating in NFL history (104.9 entering 2014). The passer rating takes into account a player's passing attempts, yards, completions, touchdowns, and interceptions. Rodgers was at his best in the 2011 season. Coming off a Super Bowl win, he threw 45 touchdowns and only six interceptions for a QB rating of 122.5 — the highest single-season rating in NFL history.

Who is the only player to win two Heisman Trophies?

If you are a college football player, what's better than winning the Heisman Trophy, the award given every year to the best player in the college game? Answer: Winning it twice. Only one player has ever done that: Ohio State running back **Archie Griffin.**

Griffin won the Heisman as a junior in 1974 and as senior in '75. In his junior year, he ran for 1,620 yards in 11 regular-season games; the following year, he ran for 1,357 in the same span. After his college career, Griffin played seven seasons with the Cincinnati Bengals. Adjusting to the pro game proved tough — Griffin never cracked 700 yards in an NFL season.

Who has won the most Super Bowl MVP awards?

Joe Montana, the legendary quarterback of the San Francisco 49ers throughout the 1980s and into the early '90s, performed under pressure better than any QB in the history of the game. It's why his nickname was Joe Cool. While other players panicked when big games were on the line, Montana calmly went about the business of winning four Super Bowls for the 49ers. In his career, Montana was named MVP of three Super Bowls — XVI in 1982, XIX in 1985, and XXIV in 1990, more than any other player in the history of the game.

SUPER STAT:

★ 39 ★

Number of touchdowns Sanders scored in 1988, a single-season NCAA record that was tied by Wisconsin's Montee Ball in 2011

FAST FACT:
BARRY SANDERS SET THE SINGLE-GAME NCAA RUSHING RECORD WITH 332 YARDS AGAINST TEXAS TECH ON DECEMBER 3, 1988, HOURS AFTER LEARNING HE HAD WON THE HEISMAN TROPHY.

Who has the most rushing yards in one NCAA season?

Using stats is one way to measure a player's greatness. Let's take a look at the numbers put up by running back **Barry Sanders.** As a junior at Oklahoma State in the 1988 season, he ran for 2,682 yards in only 11 games — the most rushing yards in an NCAA season. Sanders was drafted third overall by the Detroit Lions in 1989 and went on to have the kind of career players dream of: 10 Pro Bowls, an NFL MVP award, 14 consecutive 100-yard games (an NFL record), and more than 10,000 rushing yards in his career. He is one of only seven men to ever run for 2,000 yards in an NFL season.

But stats don't tell you how Barry Sanders ran the football. He was the most elusive player in the history of the game. After taking the handoff, he danced through piles of players before bursting free. He ran around players. He spun, he juked, and he cut on a dime. Sanders surprised the world when he abruptly retired from the NFL before the 1999 season — after all, he had run for 1,491 yards the year before and was still one of the game's elite backs. But Sanders was ready to bow out while still at the top of his game, leaving behind a highlight reel of some of the greatest plays in history.

GOLF

4

Who has the most dominant Major win in PGA history?

Tiger Woods started playing when he was 2 years old growing up in California. He even appeared on network TV at that age to show off his awesome skills. Before he was 10, he was beating adults. Eleven years later, at the age of 21, he became the youngest player — and the first African-American — to win the Masters.

How good is Tiger? He entered 2014 with 79 PGA tour wins and 14 victories in Majors — only Jack Nicklaus has won more Majors. Woods has been named the PGA Player of the Year a record 11 times, including in 2013. His most dominant win in a Major came on June 18, 2000, when Woods won the U.S. Open by an unprecedented 15 strokes in Pebble Beach, California.

Despite all he has achieved, Woods still wants to improve — and that's what makes him a true champion. "You can always get better and that's the exciting part," he said.

SUPER STAT:

★ **281** ★

Record number of consecutive weeks Woods spent as the world's top-ranked player, from June 2005 to October 2010

★ **59** ★

Second-round score Sorenstam shot on March 16, 2001 — she's the only woman to shoot under 60 in an LPGA tournament

Who has won the most LPGA Player of the Year honors?

Winning didn't always come easy to **Annika Sorenstam.** As a junior player growing up in Sweden, Sorenstam was very shy. So shy, in fact, that she would deliberately miss shots on the final hole to avoid having to give a victory speech at the end of the tournament. She'd have to get used to it, though. During her career, Sorenstam became one of the greatest female golfers in history, winning 72 LPGA tournaments. That's a lot of post-tournament speeches to give.

Sorenstam dominated women's golf for a decade, starting in the mid-'90s. She was named the LPGA Tour Player of the Year eight times — in 1995, '97, '98, 2001, '02, '03, '04, and '05 — which is more than any other player in history.

How did Sorenstam overcome her shyness? Her coaches noticed that she might be missing shots on purpose to avoid talking in public, so they made a rule that the runner-up had to give a speech, too. Sorenstam figured that if she had to talk to the crowd, she might as well do it as a champion.

Who is the golfer with the most Major championships?

It's no surprise that the player with the most Majors is also considered the greatest golfer of all time. Meet **Jack Nicklaus,** whose 18 career victories in Majors is more than any other player. (Tiger Woods entered 2014 ranked second, with 14.) Nicklaus also holds the record for the most number of Masters wins, with six.

Nicknamed the Golden Bear, Nicklaus, along with Arnold Palmer and Gary Player, was an important figure in golf's rise in popularity during the 1960s and '70s. His competitive fire and mental toughness were as much of an asset as his swing and putting skills. For his achievements, Nicklaus was named the PGA Player of the Year five times between 1967 and '76. No wonder Tiger Woods grew up with a poster of Jack Nicklaus on his bedroom wall.

Who has the lowest score in U.S. Open history?

The record for the lowest — meaning the best — score in U.S. Open history was set in 2011 when **Rory McIlroy** of Northern Ireland won by shooting 16 strokes under par. He finished eight strokes ahead of second-place finisher Jason Day in a display of almost flawless golf. The following year, McIlroy added a PGA Championship to his achievements and became the Number 1 golfer in the world. He was named the PGA Player of the Year in 2012.

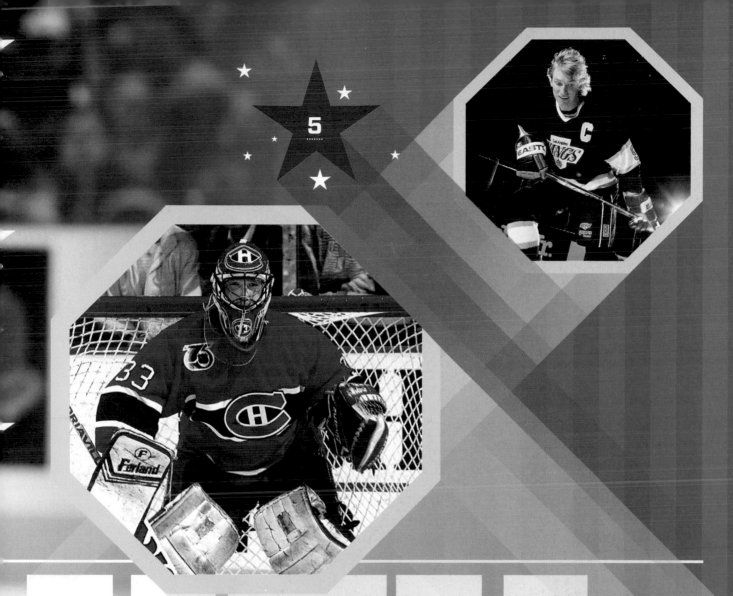

KEY

5

Who has won the most Conn Smythe Trophies?

The Conn Smythe Trophy is awarded each spring to the Most Valuable Player of the NHL's Stanley Cup playoffs, and goaltender **Patrick Roy** is the only player ever to win the award three times. He was just 20 years old when he capped his rookie season of 1985–86 by becoming the youngest starting netminder ever to win the Stanley Cup — his Montreal Canadiens beat the Calgary Flames in that season's finals. Roy won his second Conn Smythe Trophy seven seasons later after his Canadiens defeated Wayne Gretzky's Los Angeles Kings in the Stanley Cup Finals.

Roy was a member of the Colorado Avalanche when he won his third Conn Smythe Trophy, in 2001. The Avalanche needed to win the final two games of the seven-game Stanley Cup Final series after having lost three of the first five to the New Jersey Devils. "It's your job to figure out how to get us a goal, because I'm not letting in any," Roy told his coach, Bob Hartley, prior to Game 6. True to his word, Roy blanked the Devils, 4–0, in Game 6. Two nights later, the Avalanche won the Cup with a 3–1 victory in Game 7.

SUPER STAT:

★ 151 ★

Number of Stanley Cup playoff games Roy won during his career, which is the most post-season wins ever by a goalie

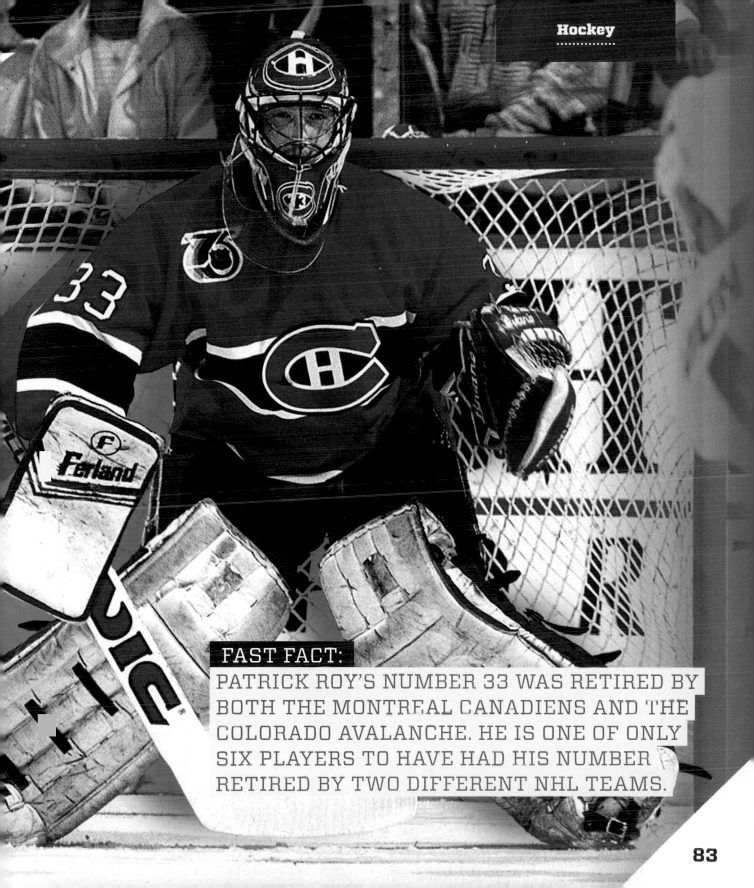

FAST FACT:
PATRICK ROY'S NUMBER 33 WAS RETIRED BY BOTH THE MONTREAL CANADIENS AND THE COLORADO AVALANCHE. HE IS ONE OF ONLY SIX PLAYERS TO HAVE HAD HIS NUMBER RETIRED BY TWO DIFFERENT NHL TEAMS.

Who holds the NHL's all-time record for most career points?

When **Wayne Gretzky** was 11 years old in 1972, he met hockey legend Gordie Howe at a sports awards banquet. Howe gave young Wayne a piece of advice: Work on your backhand. When Gretzky took the puck on that backhand and flipped it into the net with 53 seconds left in the Los Angeles Kings' game against the Edmonton Oilers on October 15, 1989, he broke the NHL career scoring record of 1,850 points that Howe built over 26 seasons.

Gretzky's momentous shot not only broke Howe's record, it also tied the game, 4–4. He then won the game for the Kings in overtime with another goal, and he did all this against his old teammates, in the city where he led the Oilers to four Stanley Cup titles before being traded to Los Angeles in 1988. Gretzky would retire in 1999 with 2,857 career points — 1,007 more than Howe recorded during his NHL career.

SUPER STAT:

★ 894 ★

The number of goals Gretzky scored to go along with his 1,963 career assists, both of which are all-time NHL records

Who is the only NHL player to captain two different teams to a championship?

Mark Messier twice won the Stanley Cup as his team's captain. The first time was in 1990, when his Edmonton Oilers defeated the Boston Bruins in the Finals. Four years later, Messier captained the New York Rangers in their Finals triumph over the Vancouver Canucks. It was the Rangers' first Cup win in 54 years, and the team has not won one since. Messier scored a goal in his final NHL game on March 31, 2004, giving him 694 for his career to go along with 1,193 assists. His 1,887 career points is second in NHL history to Wayne Gretzky.

Who played the most NHL regular-season games?

Gordie Howe played 1,767 regular-season NHL games over 26 seasons, which is more than anyone else in history. He played the first 1,687 of those games with the Detroit Red Wings from 1946 to '71. He then played one final NHL season when he suited up for 80 games as a member of the Hartford Whalers during the 1979–80 season.

Howe became known as "Mr. Hockey" while leading the Red Wings to four Stanley Cup titles during his time in Detroit. He was awarded the Hart Trophy as the league's Most Valuable Player six times. He was also a six-time winner of the Art Ross Trophy, which is given to the NHL's points leader. Howe was inducted into the Hockey Hall of Fame in 1972. He was joined there 39 years later by his son, Mark, who was inducted in 2011 after his own excellent NHL career.

Who is the most recent three-time Hart Trophy winner?

The Hart Trophy is an annual award given to the NHL player judged to be the most valuable to his team. Ever since it was first awarded after the 1923–24 season, eight players have won the Hart Trophy more than twice. The most recent of those players is **Alex Ovechkin** of the Washington Capitals. Ovechkin won the Hart Trophy for a third time in 2013 — he also won it in both 2008 and '09, and he is the only active player to have won it at least three times. (The Hart Trophy is named in honor of Dr. David Hart, who donated the trophy to the NHL. He was the father of a former Montreal Canadiens coach named Cecil Hart.)

Ovechkin's third Hart Trophy was especially impressive because he switched positions, from left wing to right wing, prior to the start of the season. He failed to score in any of his first four games, which was the longest he had ever gone without a goal at the start of an NHL season. But Ovechkin didn't give up, and he soon got the hang of playing right wing. He ended up leading the league in goals, just as he did the first two times he won the Hart Trophy.

SUPER STAT:

★ 65 ★

The number of goals Ovechkin scored during the 2007–08 regular season, which is the most ever by an NHL left winger

Who is the only NHL player to score "all five ways" in one game?

There are five kinds of goals a hockey player can score: 1) on a power play; 2) when his team is short-handed during the opposing team's power play; 3) when teams are playing at even strength; 4) on a penalty shot; and 5) into an empty net. In a game against the New Jersey Devils on December 31, 1988, **Mario Lemieux** of the Pittsburgh Penguins became the only NHL player ever to score all five of those ways in one game.

Lemieux scored three of his five goals in the first period. He first scored with the teams at even strength, then while the Devils were on a power play. He scored for a third time in the period when the Penguins were on a power play. Lemieux scored on a penalty shot in the second period. Then, when the Devils replaced their goalie with an extra skater late in the third period in a desperate attempt to score a tying goal, Lemieux made history. He scored into an empty net with just one second remaining in the game.

SUPER STAT:

★ **13** ★

Number of goals Lemieux scored during the 1988–89 season while his team was short-handed, the most ever in one season

SUPER STAT:

★ **51** ★

Number of goals Crosby scored in 2009–10, which tied him for the NHL lead with the Tampa Bay Lightning's Steven Stamkos

FAST FACT:
SIDNEY CROSBY WEARS JERSEY NUMBER 87 BECAUSE HE WAS BORN ON AUGUST 7, 1987, WHICH CAN BE WRITTEN AS 8/7/87.

Who was the NHL's youngest scoring champ?

People don't call **Sidney Crosby** of the Pittsburgh Penguins "Sid The Kid" for nothing. With 120 points on 36 goals and 84 assists during the 2006–07 NHL season, Crosby led the league in scoring when he was only 19 years old. That made him the youngest scoring champion not only in the history of the sport, but also the youngest player and the only teenager ever to win a scoring title in any major North American sports league.

Crosby would go on to be named captain of the Penguins before the start of the 2007–08 season. He led the team to the 2008 Stanley Cup Finals, where the Penguins were defeated in six games by the Detroit Red Wings. When Pittsburgh returned to the Finals against Detroit the following year, the Penguins won in seven games. Crosby became the youngest captain in NHL history to win the Stanley Cup.

Crosby was born in the Canadian city of Halifax. He scored the game-winning goal for Canada in overtime of the gold medal game at the 2010 Olympics. Four years later, he was the captain of the Canadian team that won the gold medal at the 2014 Olympics.

Who was the first American forward to win the Conn Smythe Trophy?

When **Patrick Kane** of the Chicago Blackhawks won the Conn Smythe Trophy as the Most Valuable Player of the 2013 Stanley Cup playoffs, he became the first American-born forward ever to do so. He grew up in Buffalo, New York, and was drafted first overall by Chicago in 2007. Kane became a star right away, being named NHL Rookie of the Month for October 2007 after tallying 5 goals and 11 assists in his first 12 NHL games. His MVP performance in the 2013 playoffs helped the Blackhawks win their second Stanley Cup title in four years.

Who has the most points in a season by an NHL defenseman?

The 139 points **Bobby Orr** tallied on 37 goals and 102 assists in 1970–71 is the highest point total ever by an NHL defenseman in one season. During a 12-year NHL career that began in 1966 and ended in 1978, Orr twice led the league in scoring, in 1969–70 and again in 1974–75 — he remains the only defenseman ever to lead the NHL in scoring. He also twice led the Boston Bruins to Stanley Cup titles, in 1970 and '72. He dominated the New York Rangers in the 1972 Stanley Cup Finals despite playing on a severely injured knee. Orr scored his second Stanley Cup-winning goal and was awarded the Conn Smythe Trophy as the playoff MVP — the first player to win the award twice.

Who has the most wins as a goalie?

New Jersey Devils goalie **Martin Brodeur** made 30 saves in his team's 3–2 victory over the Chicago Blackhawks on March 17, 2009. It was the 552nd win of Brodeur's career, and it was very fitting that the win came on St. Patrick's Day — Brodeur broke the all-time NHL record of 551 wins that had been held by Hall of Famer *Patrick* Roy. Roy was Brodeur's childhood idol and was at New Jersey's Prudential Center with Brodeur's father to celebrate the moment. After the final buzzer, Brodeur cut the net off the goalposts and took a victory lap. Three nights earlier, a sold-out crowd in his hometown of Montreal had chanted his name while he tied the mark held by Roy.

Brodeur has never played for another NHL team since appearing in his first game with the Devils in 1992. He has led New Jersey to three Stanley Cup titles and won the Vezina Trophy four times as the league's top goalie. On December 21, 2009, Brodeur set another NHL record when he stopped all 35 shots in a 4–0 win over the Pittsburgh Penguins for his 104th career shutout.

SUPER STAT:

14

Number of seasons in which Brodeur has won 30 or more games, which is an all-time record for an NHL goaltender

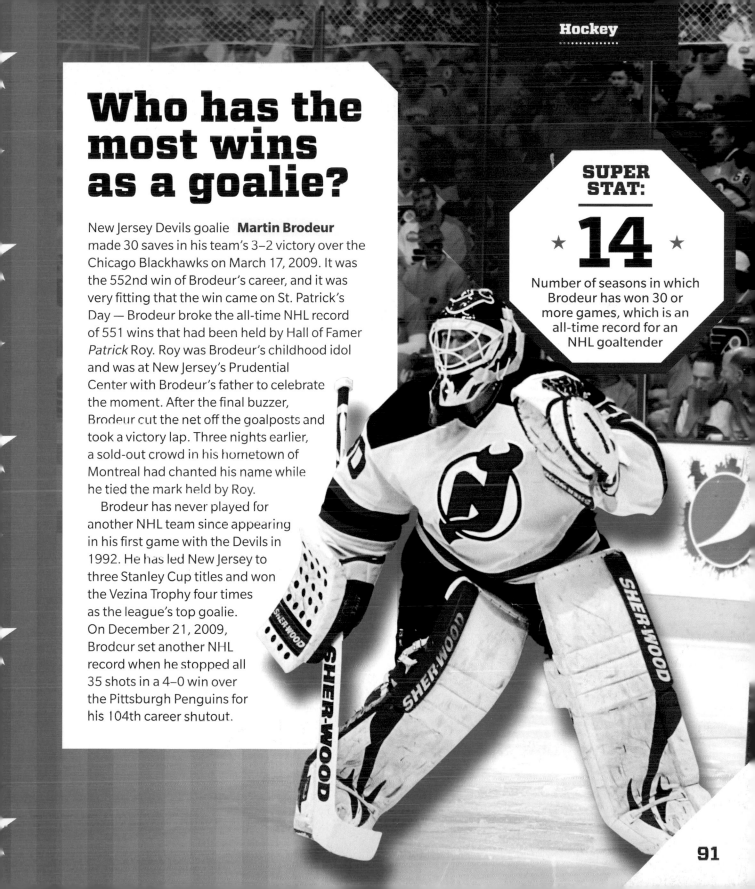

OLYM

6

FAST FACT:
GABBY DOUGLAS APPEARED
AS A GUEST IN A 2013
EPISODE OF A DISNEY XD
SERIES CALLED *KICKIN' IT.*

SUPER
STAT:

★.259★

The point total by which Douglas
beat silver-medalist Viktoria
Komova of Russia in the 2012
Olympics individual
all-around event

Who is the first American gymnast to win an individual and a team gold medal at the same Olympic Games?

For gymnast **Gabby Douglas,** sacrifice paid off. Big time. At the 2012 London Olympics, Douglas, at age 16, became the first U.S. gymnast to win an individual and a team gold medal at the same Games. Douglas won the individual all-around, in which each athlete competes in four disciplines — the vault, uneven bars, balance beam, and floor. She also won gold in the team competition, along with her Fierce Five teammates, Aly Raisman, McKayla Maroney, Kyla Ross, and Jordyn Wieber.

Douglas's road to Olympic gold was not an easy one, though. She moved away from her family in Virginia Beach, Virginia, at the age of 14 to train with legendary coach Liang Chow in West Des Moines, Iowa. Originally her mom said no way to Douglas leaving home (and moving halfway across the country), but her older sisters convinced her otherwise. Douglas missed her family, but she never gave up her dream.

Who is the fastest woman of all time?

Sports had never seen a figure like **Florence Griffith-Joyner.** At the 1988 Olympics, Flo Jo brought swagger and style to the track — colorful outfits and four-inch fingernails were her trademarks.

But Griffith-Joyner was much more than flash. She also had blazing speed and is the fastest woman in history. In 1988, she set a world record in the 100-meter sprint at the U.S. Olympic trials in Indianapolis, Indiana, with a time of 10.49 seconds — a record that still stands all these years later. At the 1988 Seoul Games, she won three gold medals and set a record in the 200 meters with a time of 21.34 seconds, a mark that also still stands.

Who stole the show at the heated 1936 Olympic Games?

Sports can be about a lot more than wins, losses, and records. Case in point: the performances of U.S. track and field superstar **Jesse Owens** at the 1936 Olympics.

The Games were held in Berlin, Germany, three years before the outbreak of World War II. The leader of Germany was Adolf Hitler, who believed that black and Jewish athletes shouldn't be allowed to compete. Facing boycotts from other countries, he relented and thought that Aryan athletes — whites, whom Hitler thought to be racially superior — would win regardless.

Owens proved Hitler and his racist ideas wrong. He won four gold medals, in the 100 meters, 200 meters, long jump, and 4x100m relay. His feat would not be equaled until the 1984 Olympics, when Carl Lewis took gold in the same four events. Every year, USA Track and Field, the sport's governing body, gives the Jesse Owens Award to the country's top track and field athlete. Recipients of the award may run faster or jump farther than Owens did, but none have made a statement as important.

Who was the first woman to win a downhill skiing gold medal for the U.S.?

Lindsey Vonn is the most successful U.S. skier of all time. At the 2010 Vancouver Olympics, she became the first U.S. woman ever to win downhill gold. Vonn also took home bronze in the Super-G discipline.

Vonn grew up in the greater Minneapolis, Minnesota, area and was skiing by the age of 2. At the 2006 Games in Turin, Italy, she crashed on a training run and had to be taken to the hospital in a helicopter. Despite the pain, Vonn got out of bed and returned to the slopes two days later, finishing eighth in the downhill competition. The comeback proved just how unstoppable she would be. Two years later, Vonn made history when she became only the second U.S. women's skier to take home the overall World Cup title. By 2012, she had won three more overall titles and had 13 World Cup wins.

FAST FACT:
LINDSEY VONN WAS OFFERED MONEY OR A COW WHEN SHE WON THE 2005 WORLD CUP DOWNHILL IN VAL D'ISERE, FRANCE. SHE CHOSE THE COW AND NAMED IT OLYMPE.

FAST FACT:
MICHAEL PHELPS WAS NAMED 2008 SPORTSMAN OF THE YEAR BY *SPORTS ILLUSTRATED*.

SUPER STAT:

★ **24** ★

Number of events in which Phelps competed during his Olympic career — he won a medal in all but two of them

Who is the most decorated athlete ever in the Olympics?

When he started swimming at the age of 7, **Michael Phelps** didn't like to put his face in the water. His solution? Swim backstroke instead. Fast-forward two decades, and he has more Olympic medals to his name than anyone in history. During his career, Michael Phelps won 22 Olympic medals. He won eight in 2004 in Athens, another eight — all of them gold — in 2008 in Beijing, and six in 2012 in London. And not one of them was for backstroke.

Of his 22 medals, 18 are gold — double the second-highest career gold-medal haul in history. By any measure, Phelps is the greatest Olympian ever. His performance in Beijing in 2008 was the stuff of legend, with his eight gold medals as the most ever won at a single Olympics. His most incredible feat was winning gold in the men's 4x200m freestyle relay less than an hour after winning gold in the 200m butterfly. After winning his eight golds, Phelps said, "It's a very hard thing to accomplish. I think it shows whatever you put your mind to, you really can accomplish."

Who was drafted by both the Chicago Bulls and the Dallas Cowboys in the same year?

Was it a college football star? No. A hoops standout? No. In fact, it was someone known for a completely different sport. In 1984, track and field legend **Carl Lewis** was drafted by the Chicago Bulls and the Dallas Cowboys, but he never played for either team. He won four gold medals in the Los Angeles Olympics later that year in the 100 meters, 200 meters, 4x100, and long jump to become the world's biggest track and field star for years to come.

Michael Jordan was selected third overall by the NBA's Bulls in 1984; Lewis was drafted 208th overall and in the 10th round. The NFL's Cowboys picked Lewis in the 12th round. Lewis, wisely, stuck with what he knew — running and jumping, very fast and very far. He won 10 Olympic medals in his career. Nine of them were gold, including victory in the long jump at the 1996 Games in Atlanta, 12 years after his Olympic debut. He won gold in the long jump in four straight Olympics. Lewis was named the athlete of the century by the International Association of Athletics Federations.

SUPER STAT:

19.80

Number of seconds in which Lewis ran the 200-meter event at the 1984 Games, which broke the previous Olympic record

Who has won the most medals among U.S. Winter Olympians?

In February 1994, **Apolo Ohno** was doing what any sports-loving 12-year-old would be doing: He was glued to the Winter Olympics taking place in Lillehammer, Norway. And when he saw short-track speedskating for the first time, Ohno knew he wanted to do what he saw unfolding on the screen: Guys, as he put it, who wore samurai swords for skates, leaning at impossible angles, and moving at 40 miles an hour. Ohno would go on to do that better than any other American.

At 13, he started training at the Lake Placid Olympic Training Center. He won his first national title at the age of 14. Eight years after he first saw the sport on TV, Ohno won his first Olympic gold in Salt Lake City in 2002. Ohno would compete in three Olympic Games and win a total of eight medals, including two gold to become the most decorated U.S. Winter Olympic athlete of all time.

SUPER STAT:

133.7

Number of seconds in which Ohno skated 1,500 meters at the 2001 Olympic trials to set a world short-track speedskating record

Who is the first woman to compete in seven swimming events at one Olympics?

At the London Games, 17-year-old **Missy Franklin** became the first woman to compete in seven swimming events at one Olympics. She won the 100-meter and 200-meter backstroke, the 4x200m freestyle relay, and the 4x100m medley relay. Nicknamed Missy the Missile, she started swimming at the age of 5; her dad calls her now-size 13 feet "built-in flippers." After winning five medals at the 2012 London Olympics, including four golds, Franklin returned home and continued to swim for her high school, Regis Jesuit. Good luck trying to beat her.

Who was the first high jumper to flop backward over the bar?

Before **Dick Fosbury,** high jumpers would jump over the bar forward or kick their legs over like a pair of scissors. Fosbury changed that — and his sport — forever. What Fosbury did was revolutionary, and it's why the most common style of high jumping, in which the athlete falls backward over the bar, is called the Fosbury Flop.

Growing up in Portland, Oregon, Fosbury wasn't succeeding in the sport he loved by using the existing techniques, so he made up his own. He ran in diagonally, then curved in as he made his final approach, before leaping backward over the bar and landing on his back. His new method gained attention, and not all of it was good. In 1964, a newspaper ran a photo of Fosbury's back-first style with the caption: "World's Laziest High Jumper." Fosbury was unfazed. He won the gold medal and set an Olympic record in the high jump at the 1968 Summer Olympics in Mexico City with a leap of 2.24 meters. Today, no one laughs at Fosbury's method. Everyone uses it.

SUPER STAT:

37.10

Number of seconds in which Bolt's Jamaican team ran the 4x100m relay at the 2008 Games to set an Olympic record

Who is the fastest man in the world?

Jamaican sprinter **Usain Bolt** is known for his cool, laidback style. But he does get nervous. Before the World Junior Championships in 2002, the then-15-year-old Bolt was so jumpy before competing in front of his hometown crowd in Kingston, Jamaica, he put his running shoes on the wrong feet before the race. He still won.

Bolt has only gotten swifter since, earning the title of fastest man on the planet. At the 2009 World Championships in Berlin, Germany, Bolt set the 100-meter record with a time of 9.58 seconds. That's a speed of 23.355 miles per hour! He broke the world record in the 200m, with a time of 19.19 seconds, at the same event. Lightning Bolt also has six Olympic gold medals to his name — three in Beijing and three in London in 2012, all in the 100m, 200m, and the men's 4x100m relay.

RACING

Who is the only driver to win five straight NASCAR season championships?

NASCAR drivers have spent most of the past several years trying to catch **Jimmie Johnson.** Few of them have succeeded. Johnson is the most dominant driver in the sport today — and he's the only driver to win five straight Championships. At the end of the 2006, '07, '08, '09, and '10 seasons, Johnson hoisted the Cup Trophy while his competition watched. He then claimed his sixth Championship in 2013.

What makes Johnson so good? NASCAR is a team sport — and Johnson's Hendrick Motorsports team is the best in the business. Johnson's cars have been fast and reliable, which is crucial for a driver to have a chance at winning. Then there's Johnson himself. He has all of the skills to be a great driver — quick reaction times, hand-eye coordination, and the ability to know how to get the best out of his car.

SUPER STAT:

★ **4** ★

The record number of times Johnson won the NASCAR Sprint Cup Series All-Star race, in 2003, '06, '12, and '13

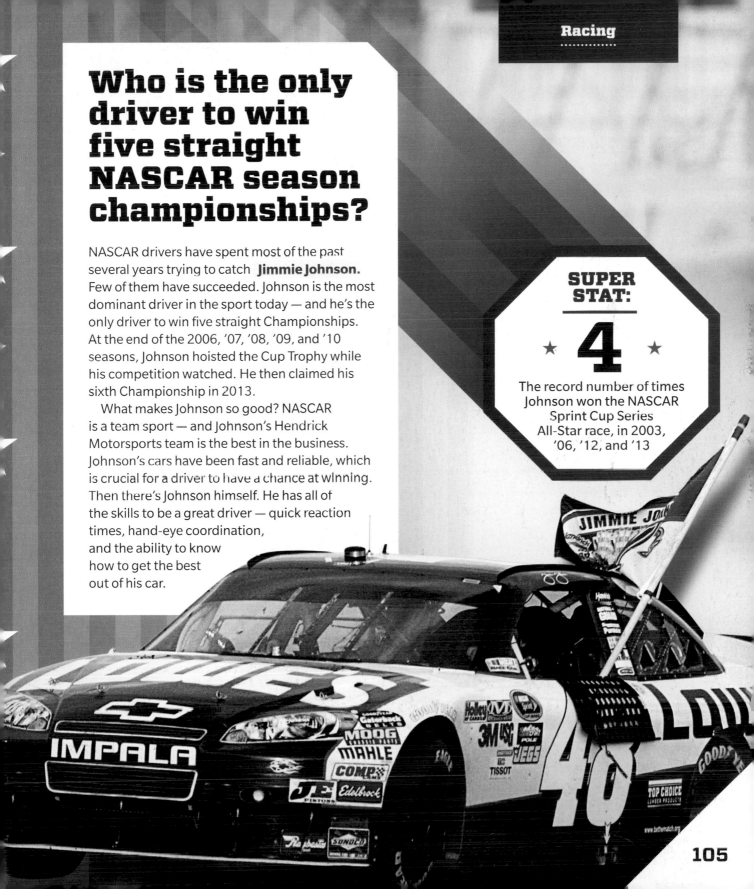

Who is the first female driver to win a NASCAR Cup Series pole position?

What's green, has four wheels, and just zoomed past at more than 196 mph? That'd be **Danica Patrick's** Number 10 Chevrolet in the qualifying round of the 2013 Daytona 500. Her lap time of 45.817 seconds earned her pole position for NASCAR's biggest race of the season, making her the first woman to win a NASCAR Cup Series pole position.

Don't tell Patrick that women shouldn't race cars. She's been lapping the competition since she was a girl growing up in Illinois. Her big break came in 2005 when she started driving in the IndyCar series — she earned Rookie of the Year honors in her first season. In 2008, she won the Indy Japan 300, the first win ever by a woman in the IndyCar Series.

Who is the only driver to win the Indianapolis 500, Daytona 500, and Formula One World Championship?

Retired racing legend **Mario Andretti** never met a race car he didn't like. Or one he couldn't make go very, very fast. He's the only driver in history to win the Indianapolis 500, the Daytona 500, and the Formula One World Championship. That's three of the biggest titles in racing in three very different types of cars.

Andretti's love of automobiles goes back to when he was a boy growing up in Italy after World War II. At 13, he took a job parking cars at a local garage. Andretti and his family migrated to the U.S. in 1955 and four years later he was racing in local events near his new hometown of Nazareth, Pennsylvania. His career flourished — he went on to win NASCAR's Daytona 500 in 1967, the open-wheel Indianapolis 500 in 1967, and the Formula One Drivers' Championship in 1978.

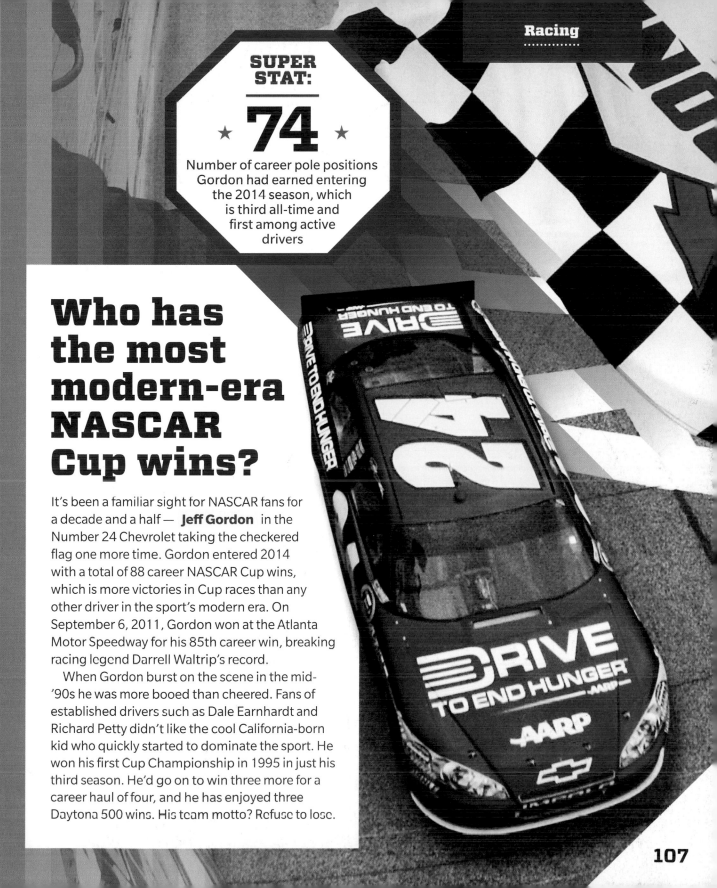

SUPER STAT:

★ **74** ★

Number of career pole positions
Gordon had earned entering
the 2014 season, which
is third all-time and
first among active
drivers

Who has the most modern-era NASCAR Cup wins?

It's been a familiar sight for NASCAR fans for a decade and a half — **Jeff Gordon** in the Number 24 Chevrolet taking the checkered flag one more time. Gordon entered 2014 with a total of 88 career NASCAR Cup wins, which is more victories in Cup races than any other driver in the sport's modern era. On September 6, 2011, Gordon won at the Atlanta Motor Speedway for his 85th career win, breaking racing legend Darrell Waltrip's record.

   When Gordon burst on the scene in the mid-'90s he was more booed than cheered. Fans of established drivers such as Dale Earnhardt and Richard Petty didn't like the cool California-born kid who quickly started to dominate the sport. He won his first Cup Championship in 1995 in just his third season. He'd go on to win three more for a career haul of four, and he has enjoyed three Daytona 500 wins. His team motto? Refuse to lose.

SOC

CER

SUPER
STAT:

★ **49** ★

Number of goals Ronaldo scored
in international competition
entering the 2014 World Cup,
the most ever by a
Portuguese player

FAST FACT:
CRISTIANO RONALDO BECAME THE
FIRST TOP EUROPEAN LEAGUE PLAYER
TO REACH 40 GOALS IN TWO CONSECUTIVE
SEASONS, IN 2010–11 AND '11–12.

Who has won the European Golden Shoe in two different leagues?

Portuguese soccer player **Cristiano Ronaldo** has been awarded the European Golden Shoe twice for being Europe's leading goalscorer in top-division club matches — and he has done it with different clubs and in different leagues. In the 2010–11 season, Ronaldo scored 40 goals for Spanish powerhouse Real Madrid. Three years before that, in 2007–08, he scored 31 goals in the English Premier League for Manchester United. He's the only player in history to win the award twice in two different leagues.

What makes Ronaldo so good? It's a long list. He's a ruthless finisher when he has a chance to score a goal. He has great pace and ball skills that allow him to dribble past defenders to set up a shot on goal, or to make a great pass to set up a teammate. He's a great header of the ball. And he's good with his left foot and with his right foot, making him a double threat for nervous goalkeepers.

SUPER STAT:

★ **35** ★

Seconds it took Dempsey to score on September 7, 2012, against Jamaica, the fastest U.S. goal ever in World Cup qualifying

Who was named U.S. men's team captain during qualifying for the 2014 World Cup?

When he was a 15-year-old growing up in Nacogdoches, Texas, **Clint Dempsey** used to play against grown men twice his size in local league matches. He loved to use the dribbling and ball-control tricks he would see Diego Maradona of Argentina, his idol, make to baffle his bigger, more-experienced opponents. With every successful trick move they fell for, the adult players looked ever-more foolish, as the young Dempsey sped past them to score another goal.

Fast-forward 15 years and that kid from Nacogdoches was named the captain of the U.S. men's national team for a 2014 World Cup qualifying game against Costa Rica. Come game time, a blizzard covered the field in snow. The U.S. won the game 1–0 and got a spot in the World Cup.

Dempsey has been on the U.S. squad since 2004, playing in 101 matches and scoring 36 goals. He's second on the all-time U.S. men's goal scoring list, behind Landon Donovan, who has 57. He has played in England for Premier League sides Fulham and Tottenham Hotspur; in 2013, he returned to the U.S. and signed with the Seattle Sounders of the MLS. Dempsey is known for his ability to improvise and innovate on the pitch, taking chances that other players won't. Just like he did when he was a kid.

Who has the record for the latest goal by a member of the U.S. women's national team?

Alex Morgan's game-winning header in the 123rd minute of the 2012 London Olympics semifinal against Canada is the latest goal ever scored by a member of the U.S. women's national team. In the dying moments of extra time, Morgan found space in the box and got on the end of a pass to give the U.S. a 4–3 lead. The win advanced the Americans to the Olympic final, where the U.S. won a gold medal with a 2–1 victory over Japan.

Who is the greatest soccer player of all time?

Debating sports with friends is fun. Everyone has an opinion on who ranks where and why. And those opinions are rarely unanimous — except when it comes to soccer. **Pelé,** who played for Brazil 92 times from 1957 to '71, is universally hailed as the greatest player ever.

Pelé's Brazilian teams won three World Cups in dominating fashion. He scored a record 1,281 goals throughout his career. He had it all: speed, vision, athleticism, and balance.

Pelé grew up poor. His family could not even afford a soccer ball, so as a boy, he played with a sock stuffed with newspapers or grapefruits. In 1978, Pelé received the International Peace Award, and in retirement he's worked with the UN and UNICEF to promote peace. Pelé's greatest achievement may be putting as much effort into being a humanitarian as he did into becoming the greatest soccer player ever.

FAST FACT:
IN 2013, MIA HAMM BECAME
THE FIRST WOMAN TO BE
INDUCTED INTO THE WORLD
FOOTBALL HALL OF FAME
IN PACHUCA, MEXICO.

Who was the first female soccer superstar?

Before Abby Wambach, Alex Morgan, and Hope Solo took center stage for the U.S. women's soccer team, there was **Mia Hamm** — the first female soccer superstar on the planet. She is the greatest player in the history of women's soccer and she inspired many girls to play the game.

Hamm played at a level no one had ever seen before in women's soccer. She represented the U.S. 275 times and scored 158 goals. When she retired in 2004, she held the record for most goals scored by any man or woman in international soccer. In her four seasons at the University of North Carolina, starting in 1989, Hamm's teams won four NCAA women's soccer titles. In fact, during those four seasons, Hamm's team only lost once in the 95 games she played. In 1991, the U.S. won the World Cup, with 19-year-old Hamm leading the way. Eight years after that, Hamm won another World Cup for the U.S. She also has two Olympic gold medals and a silver. At her final Olympics in Athens in 2004, Hamm was chosen by her fellow Olympians to carry the U.S. flag at the closing ceremony. It was a fitting end to the career of the soccer superstar.

SUPER STAT:

★ 103 ★

Number of goals Hamm scored at the University of North Carolina, the most ever by a woman in Atlantic Coast Conference history

Who won the first three FIFA Ballon d'Or honors?

The FIFA Ballon d'Or — that's French for "Golden Ball"— is the award given every year to the best soccer player in the world by the sport's international governing body, FIFA. The winner is determined by votes from coaches and captains of international teams and from soccer reporters around the globe. It debuted in 2010 after *France Football*'s Ballon d'Or and the men's FIFA World Player of the Year award were merged. In its first three years, it was awarded to the same player every time: Argentina's **Lionel Messi.**

Messi plays for Barcelona in Spain's La Liga, one of the toughest leagues in international soccer. But his road to soccer glory didn't come easily. Messi moved to Spain from Argentina at the age of 13 after being diagnosed with a growth hormone deficiency in his bones. The treatments were very expensive, but Barcelona promised to pay for Messi's medicine if he moved to Spain to join the team's junior training academy. He did — and he's been with the club ever since.

What makes Messi so good? He's lightning fast, he's very tough to tackle, he has amazing ball control that allows him to dribble past defenders, and he's a great teammate who knows how and when to perfectly pass the ball so that others can score.

SUPER STAT:

★ 50 ★

Number of goals Messi scored for Barcelona in 2011–12, which is the most ever by a player in a single La Liga season

Who was employed as Manchester United's mascot years before becoming their star player?

English soccer legend **David Beckham** made his Premier League debut at 10 years old. Well, sort of. He didn't score any goals or even kick the ball, because he was busy working as the team mascot for Manchester United.

Four years later, he signed a playing contract with the club. He went on to play 265 games for Man U, scoring 62 goals, and winning six Premier League titles. After Manchester, Beckham played for Real Madrid in Spain, the L.A. Galaxy in the U.S., and for Paris Saint-Germain in France — winning titles at every club he played for.

Beckham was famous for his skill at taking free kicks. He could send the ball bending though the air around defenders and finding the back of the net; he scored 65 goals from free kicks in his career.

SUPER STAT:

★ **3** ★

Number of different World Cups at which Beckham scored a goal (1998, 2002, and '06), the only Englishman ever to do so

TENNIS

9

Who has won the most men's tennis Grand Slam titles?

Roger Federer holds the most tennis Grand Slam titles, with a total of 17. That's a big reason why many experts think the Swiss player is the best the world has ever seen. There are four Grand Slam events in tennis — the Australian, French and U.S. Opens, plus the Wimbledon Championships. They're the toughest events in the sport and they're the hardest to win. Federer has won the Australian Open four times, the French Open once, the U.S. Open five times, and has seven Wimbledon wins.

As a player, Federer has it all. He can play at the net or on the baseline, he has a great blend of speed and power, and he never gives up. He's also a great sportsman, never bragging when he wins and never behaving like a sore loser when he doesn't.

Federer broke the previous record of 14 Grand Slam titles, held by the U.S.'s Pete Sampras, when he defeated Andy Roddick to win the 2009 Wimbledon Championship for his 15th Major. Since then, Federer has added titles at the 2010 Australian Open and 2012 Wimbledon Championships to increase his record to 17.

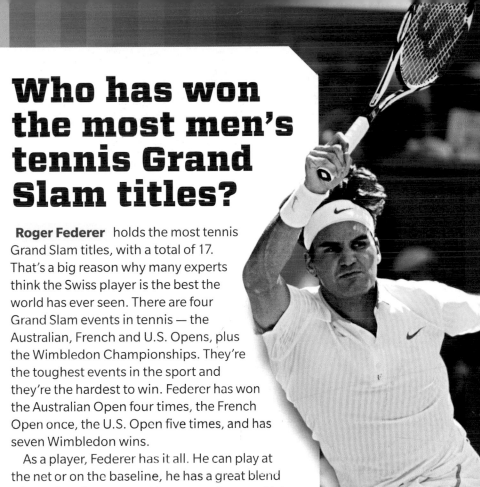

SUPER STAT:

★ **302** ★

The number of weeks Federer spent as the Number 1 men's singles player in the world, which is the most ever

Who has the longest winning streak in tennis history?

Is it Serena Williams? No. Roger Federer? Wrong. Rafa? Nope. Pete Sampras, or Monica Seles, or Steffi Graf, or Novak Djokovic? All no. The holder of the longest winning streak in tennis history is **Esther Vergeer.** The Dutch athlete won 470 consecutive wheelchair tennis matches. Wheelchair tennis is a version of the sport adapted for people with disabilities. The courts, rackets and balls are all the same, but the athletes use special wheelchairs to move around the court and the ball can bounce twice instead of once.

That's right — she won 470 straight matches. Let's put that winning streak into perspective. In the NBA, the Lakers hold the longest streak with 33 games. In 1941, Joe DiMaggio hit in 56 consecutive MLB games, a record. The Patriots won 23 games straight in the early 2000s to claim the longest winning streak in NFL history.

Who won the longest match ever played?

No matter what else he achieves in his career, U.S. tennis player **John Isner** will always be remembered as the winner of the longest match in the game's history. How long? Eleven hours and five minutes. The first-round match of the 2010 Wimbledon Championships took place over three days until the final scoreline read 6–4, 3–6, 6–7, 7–6, 70–68. It's impossible not to feel bad for Isner's opponent, Frenchman Nicolas Mahut. The reason that the last set went so long — eight hours and 11 minutes — is because there are no tiebreakers in the fifth set of matches at the Wimbledon Championships. The players have to fight it out until one of them wins by two games. Even if it takes three days.

Who is the lowest-ranked tennis player to defeat two top-10 players in one tournament?

You might not believe it but it's true: **Serena Williams** was once ranked 304th in the world in tennis. In November 1997, she entered the Ameritech Cup in Chicago as the 304th-ranked player in the world and went on to upset then-world Number 7 Mary Pierce and Number 4 Monica Seles.

In five years, Williams went from 304th to Number 1 in the world. She is the most dominant women's tennis player of her era. Williams entered 2014 with 17 Grand Slam singles titles. She holds a career Grand Slam, too (winning the Australian, French and U.S. Opens, and at Wimbledon). Along with her older sister Venus, Serena changed women's tennis, bringing more power and athleticism than anyone had seen before.

XTREME

Who was the first skateboarder to land a '900'?

During X Games V in 1999, skateboarder **Tony Hawk** landed the first-ever documented 900. What's a 900? It stands for 900 degrees, a move in which he launched off the top of the ramp, spun through two-and-a-half full rotations, and stuck the landing.

Hawk is the most important skateboarder in history. He helped turn a kids' pastime into a mainstream international sport. After turning pro at age 14, he was one of the best skaters in the world two years later. Many champions are content to sit back and enjoy their success, but Hawk has always pushed himself to test the limits of skateboarding possibility. Enter the 900 — the trick nobody had ever done. At the X Games, Hawk flamed out 10 times in a row trying, but he never gave up. One last shot. Then, finally, he landed it, and history was his.

SUPER STAT:

★ **73** ★

Number of times Hawk won in the 103 pro contests he had competed in by the age of 25

FAST FACT:
SHAUN WHITE PLAYS GUITAR
IN A BAND CALLED BAD THINGS,
WHICH RELEASED ITS FIRST
ALBUM ON JANUARY 21, 2014.

Who has won the most X Games medals?

The 23 X Games medals **Shaun White** has won since making his debut in 2003 is more than anyone else in history. Of those 23, 15 are gold, five are silver, and three are bronze. White has won 18 medals in snowboarding and five in skateboarding. He is considered by most to be the greatest board sport athlete of all time.

Before he was a year old, White underwent two major surgeries to correct a heart defect. He recovered, and by the time he was 4, he was skiing down slopes, trying to catch his older brother, Jesse, on family trips. In an attempt to try to slow Shaun down, his mom put him on a snowboard at the age of 6. Bad news for her: It only made White go faster.

Skateboarding legend Tony Hawk met White at a San Diego skate park when White was 9. With Hawk's advice and encouragement, White became a skateboarding pro at 17 and a member of Hawk's Birdhouse skate team. He also likes to surf. And he's tried his hand at rally car driving too. Whatever White does, he does it well. Or, as he puts it, "Whatever it is, be yourself."

SUPER STAT:

48.4

White's score at the 2010 Winter Olympics in the men's halfpipe, which broke the previous Olympic record he had set in 2006

Player Index

A

Aaron, Hank, 20
Abdul-Jabbar, Kareem, 33
Andretti, Mario, 106
Anthony, Carmelo, 36

B

Beckham, David, 117
Bird, Larry, 49
Bogues, Tyrone (Muggsy), 41
Bolt, Usain, 103
Brady, Tom, 60
Brees, Drew, 64
Brodeur, Martin, 91
Bryant, Kobe, 34-35

C

Cabrera, Miguel, 10-11
Cano, Robinson, 13
Chamberlain, Wilt, 32
Charles, Jamaal, 57
Crosby, Sidney, 88-89
Curry, Stephen, 49

D

Dempsey, Clint, 112
Douglas, Gabby, 94-95
Durant, Kevin, 38-39

F

Federer, Roger, 119
Foles, Nick, 56
Fosbury, Dick, 102
Franklin, Missy, 102

G

Gordon, Jeff, 107
Gordon, Josh, 67
Gretzky, Wayne, 84
Griffin, Archie, 73
Griffin, Blake, 43
Griffith-Joyner, Florence, 96
Griner, Brittney, 37

H

Hamilton, Josh, 16
Hamm, Mia, 114-115

Harper, Bryce, 16
Hawk, Tony, 123
Howard, Dwight, 48
Howe, Gordie, 85

I

Isner, John, 121

J

Jackson, Bo, 20
James, LeBron, 30-21
Jeter, Derek, 18-19
Johnson, Calvin, 58-59
Johnson, Earvin (Magic), 50
Johnson, Jimmie, 105
Jordan, Michael, 47

K

Kaepernick, Colin, 70
Kane, Patrick, 90
Kuechly, Luke, 71

L

Lemieux, Mario, 87
Lewis, Carl, 100
Luck, Andrew, 66

M

Machado, Manny, 24
Madden, John, 56
Manning, Peyton, 54-55
Maravich, Pete, 40
Mauer, Joe, 12
McIlroy, Rory, 79
Messi, Lionel, 116
Messier, Mark, 85
Montana, Joe, 73
Morgan, Alex, 113

J

Nicklaus, Jack, 79

O

Ohno, Apolo, 101
Orr, Bobby, 90

Ovechkin, Alex, 86
Owens, Jesse, 96

P

Parker, Tony, 32
Patrick, Danica, 106
Paul, Chris, 44-45
Pelé, 113
Peterson, Adrian, 62-63
Phelps, Michael, 98-99
Posey, Buster, 17
Prater, Matt, 68-69
Puig, Yasiel, 14-15
Pujols, Albert, 26-27

R

Rice, Jerry, 66
Ripken, Jr., Cal, 21
Rivera, Mariano, 6-7
Rodgers, Aaron, 72
Ronaldo, Cristiano, 110-111
Rose, Derrick, 42
Roy, Patrick, 82-83
Russell, Bill, 42
Ruth, Babe, 8
Ryan, Nolan, 24

S

Sanders, Barry, 74-75
Sanders, Delon, 9
Sorenstam, Annika, 78
Suzuki, Ichiro, 25

T

Trout, Mike, 8

V

Vergeer, Esther, 120
Verlander, Justin, 22-23
Vonn, Lindsey, 97

W

Wade, Dwyane, 46
White, Shaun, 124-125
Williams, Serena, 121
Winston, Jameis, 65
Woods, Tiger, 77
Woodson, Charles, 61

Photo Credits

Front Cover: Mike Segar/Reuters (James), Robert Beck for Sports Illustrated (Manning), Simon Bruty/Sports Illustrated (Williams), Damian Strohmeyer/Sports Illustrated (Dempsey)
Back Cover: Peter Read Miller/Sports Illustrated (Peterson), Lou Capozzola for Sports Illustrated (Crosby), John W. McDonough/Sports Illustrated (Jordan), John Biever/Sports Illustrated (Jeter)
Page 2: John W. McDonough/Sports Illustrated
Page 3: David Cannon/Getty Images (McIlroy), John Biever/Sports Illustrated (Jeter), Bob Martin for Sports Illustrated (White), John W. McDonough/Getty Images (Johnson), David Ramos/Getty Images (Messi), Lou Capozzola for Sports Illustrated (Crosby)
Page 4: John Biever/Sports Illustrated (Jeter), National Baseball Library, Cooperstown (Ruth)
Page 5: Simon Bruty/Sports Illustrated (Verlander), Rob Tringali/MLB Photos/Getty Images (Machado)
Pages 6-7: Rob Tringali/MLB Photos/Getty Images
Page 8: Robert Beck for Sports Illustrated (Trout), National Baseball Library, Cooperstown (Ruth)
Page 9: Mitchell Layton/Getty Images
Pages 10-11: Chuck Solomon/Sports Illustrated
Page 12: John Biever for Sports Illustrated
Page 13: Al Bello/Getty Images
Pages 14-15: Robert Beck/Getty Images
Page 16: Jim McIsaac/Getty Images (Hamilton), Rob Carr/Getty Images (Bryce Harper)
Page 17: Al Tielemans/Sports Illustrated
Pages 18-19: Chuck Solomon/Getty Images
Page 20: Ron Vesely/Getty Images (Jackson), MLB Photos/Getty Images (Aaron)
Page 21: Walter Iooss, Jr. for Sports Illustrated
Pages 22-23: Simon Bruty/Sports Illustrated
Page 24: Rob Tringali/MLB Photos/Getty Images (Machado), Bill Chan/AP (Nolan Ryan)
Page 25: Lisa Blumenfeld/Getty Images
Pages 26-27: John Biever/Sports Illustrated
Page 28: John W. McDonough/Sports Illustrated (James), John W. McDonough/Sports Illustrated (Griffin)
Page 29: Christophe Elise/Icon SMI (Anthony), Rich Clarkson/NCAA Photos (Maravich)
Pages 30-31: John W. McDonough/Sports illustrated
Page 32: John W. McDonough/Sports Illustrated (Parker), AP (Chamberlain)
Page 33: Focus on Sport/Getty Images
Pages 34-35: Jeff Reinking/NBAE/Getty Images
Page 36: Christophe Elise/Icon SMI
Page 37: Jim Cowsert/USA TODAY Sports
Pages 38-39: John W. McDonough/Sports Illustrated

Page 40: Rich Clarkson/NCAA Photos (Maravich)
Page 41: David E. Klutho/Sports Illustrated
Page 42: Greg Nelson For Sports Illustrated (Rose), Fred Kaplan for Sports Illustrated (Bill Russell)
Page 43: John W. McDonough/Sports Illustrated
Pages 44-45: Greg Nelson For Sports Illustrated
Page 46: Bob Rosato/Sports Illustrated
Page 47: John W. McDonough/Sports Illustrated
Page 48: Bill Frakes/Sports Illustrated
Page 49: Andy Hayt for Sports Illustrated (Bird), Sam Forencich/NBAE/Getty Images (Curry)
Page 50: Manny Millan/Sports Illustrated
Page 52: Simon Bruty/Sports Illustrated (Brady), Tony Tomsic for Sports Illustrated (Griffin), John W. McDonough/Getty Images (Johnson)
Page 53: Justin Edmonds/Getty Images (Prater)
Pages 54-55: Ezra Shaw/Getty Images
Page 56: Thearon W. Henderson/Getty Images (Foles), Neil Leifer/Sports Illustrated (John Madden)
Page 57: Jed Jacobsohn/Getty Images
Pages 58-59: John W. McDonough/Getty Images
Page 60: Simon Bruty/Sports Illustrated
Page 61: John Biever/Sports Ilustrated
Pages 62-63: Peter Read Miller/Sports Illustrated
Page 64: Robert Beck/Sports Illustrated
Page 65: Bill Frakes/Getty Images
Page 66: Jamie Squire/Getty Images (Luck), John W. McDonough/Sports Illustrated (Rice)
Page 67: Jason Miller/Getty Images
Pages 68-69: Justin Edmonds/Getty Images
Page 70: John W. McDonough/Sports Illustrated
Page 71: Streeter Lecka/Getty Images
Page 72: Al Tielemans/Getty Images
Page 73: Tony Tomsic for Sports Illustrated (Griffin), George Gojkovich/Getty Images (Montana)
Pages 74-75: Doug Hoke for Sports Illustrated
Page 76: Doug Kapustin/MCT/Getty Images (McIlroy), John Iacono/Sports Illustrated (Nicklaus)
Page 77: Elise Amendola/AP
Page 78: Scott Halleran/Getty Images
Page 79: John Iacono/Sports Illustrated (Nicklaus), David Cannon/Getty Images (McIlroy)
Page 80: B. Bennett/Getty Images (Howe), Lou Capozzola for Sports Illustrated (Crosby)
Page 81: Damian Strohmeye/Sports Illustrated (Roy), Walter Iooss Jr. for Sports Illustrated (Gretzky)

Pages 82-83: Damian Strohmeyer/Sports Illustrated
Page 84: Walter Iooss Jr. for Sports Illustrated
Page 85: B. Bennett/Getty Images (Howe), Steve Babineau/NHLI/Getty Images (Messier)
Page 86: Mike Clarke for Sports Illustrated
Page 87: B. Bennett/Getty Images
Pages 88-89: Lou Capozzola for Sports Illustrated (Sidney Crosby)
Page 90: David E. Klutho/Sports Illustrated (Kane), Tony Triolo/Sports Illustrated (Orr)
Page 91: Erick W. Rasco/Sports Illustrated
Page 92: Wide World (Owens), Simon Bruty/Sports Illustrated (Vonn)
Page 93: Peter Read Miller for Sports Illustrated (Bolt), Heinz Kluetmeier/Sports Illustrated (Franklin)
Pages 94-95: Al Tielemans/Sports Illustrated
Page 96: Manny Millan/Sports Illustrated (Griffith-Joyner), Sports Illustrated (Owens)
Page 97: Simon Bruty/Sports Illustrated
Pages 98-99: Robert Beck/Sports Illustrated
Page 100: Neil Leifer/Sports Illustrated
Page 101: Damian Strohmeyer/Sports Illustrated
Page 102: Heinz Kluetmeier/Getty Images (Franklin), Tony Duffy/Getty Images (Fosbury)
Page 103: Peter Read Miller/Sports Illustrated
Page 104: Mike Ehrmann/Getty Images (Patrick), Rusty Jarrett/Getty Images for NASCAR (Johnson)
Page 105: Chris Graythen/Getty Images
Page 106: Jerry Markland/Getty Images (Patrick), AFP/Getty Images (Mario Andretti)
Page 107: Pool/NASCAR/Getty Images (Gordon)
Page 108: Simon Bruty/Sports Illustraed (Hamm), David Ramos/Getty Images (Messi)
Page 109: Pics United/Icon SMI (Pelé), Bob Martin for Sports Illustrated (Beckham)
Pages 110-111: Christian Petersen/Getty Images
Page 112: Simon Bruty/Sports Illustrated
Page 113: Pics United/Icon SMI (Pelé), Jamie McDonald/FIFA/Getty Images (Morgan)
Pages 114-115: Simon Bruty/Sports Illustraed
Page 116: David Ramos/Getty Images
Page 117: Bob Martin for Sports Illustrated
Page 118: Oli Scarff/Getty Images (Isner), Michael S. Green/AP (Williams)
Page 119: Simon Bruty/Sports Illustrated
Page 120: Julian Finney/Getty Images
Page 121: Clive Brunskill/Getty Images (Williams), GLYN KIRK/AFP/Getty Images (Isner)
Page 122: Tony Donaldson/Icon SMI (Hawk), Bob Martin for Sports Illustrated (White)
Page 123: Tony Donaldson/Icon SMI
Pages 124-125: Bob Martin for Sports Illustrated